Make It Happen

Make It Happen

Moving Towards Your Best U!

Felicia C. Lucas

PRAISE FOR *MAKE IT HAPPEN: MOVING TOWARDS YOUR BEST U!*

"Inspired by real life events, *Make It Happen: Moving Towards Your Best U!* is a heart filled testimonial that takes you behind the remarkable journey of Author and Polishing Enthusiast, Felicia Lucas. From her relentless servanthood as a wife, mother and minister to her years of experience in corporate America, Felicia shares with you her most heart fought battles as well as some of the keys to her most amazing victories! This book is a must read for the individual who is ready to make a bold move towards living their best life ever! I know it to be true...because it has inspired me!"

-Pastor Kelvin Lucas
CEO/President Take It By Force Ministries, Inc.
www.facebook.com/takeitbyforceministries

"Where you are today in life is not your final destiny. Every day you can choose to become a better version of yourself. Living a life you love is about cultivating wholeness and happiness. Felicia Lucas has written a fantastic book to help you become joyfully whole spiritually, physically, emotionally and professionally. Her timely message will inspire you to mindfully move towards your best you and provides practical strategies to empower you to move forward and take action to become whole and happy."

-Catrice M. Jackson, International Speaker and Best-Selling Author
www.bossladyofbranding.com

"Minister Felicia has written a masterpiece using real life experiences to impart spiritual truth with a practical application. This book is a must have for anyone that desires to better their marriage relationship and a tool for those who desire to be better and move to the next level in their spiritual walk in Christ Jesus."

-Prophet Eartha Butler, Master's Touch Prophetic Ministry
www.nlrockofages.org

"Awesome and inspiring. A great collection of real world experiences that readers can relate to and learn from. This is an easy read for people entering the workforce as well as veteran workers. It is a great example of how the spiritual word can influence, encourage and enrich your personal and work life. The added bonus is the chapter and verses from the Bible are listed for you."

-Varnell Kinnin, Northeast Area Director
Friends of North Carolina Public Libraries (FONCPL)

"This is an excellent book and I did not want to put it down! I'm definitely giving this book to colleagues and friends because you share great tips on how everyone can be their best in the workplace. This book gives you all the tools you will need to succeed not only in the workplace, but in life!"

-Vickie Smith, Site Network Manager
Quintiles, Inc.

"The author's use of the analogy of the love story between her and her husband and the relationship that God desires to have with HIS people was a slam dunk. The words literally jumped off the page and painted a picture that should motivate readers to always pursue their full purpose, with their best foot forward. The book has the perfect balance of real world examples, while introducing and integrating the Holy Scriptures as evidence of the relevance of God's word in our daily lives. The transparency of the *Real Deal Talk* offers in plain language the truth regarding some of the challenges relationships may face and reinforces with God at the center, all things are possible. This book will be a blessing to singles seeking God for their mates as well as married couples that are committed to maintaining and enhancing their spousal relationships by mirroring the commitment God has made to his people!"

-Pastor Dawn Cambridge Johnson
Greater Works Community Ministries

"Felicia bursts barriers, crashes glass ceilings, eliminates excuses and provides practical principles to help every reader deal with his or her weaknesses, cultivate his or her strengths, grow into a more productive individual in all aspects of life and grow closer to God. By revealing her own real life struggles, Felicia's transparency allows the reader to connect to her and see how to apply those principles. Whether you are married or unmarried, the employer or the employee, a new Christian or a faithful soldier for Christ, this book will help you advance to your next level. Felicia not only asks provocative and insightful questions, but also provides space for the reader to write answers and jot down notes. I recommend this book to anyone who wants to change from dissatisfied to fulfilled, from average to great, and from great to exceptional."

-Denise S. Horne, Recording Artist and Registered Nurse
dkenrecords.com

"Felicia's book is a "must" read. Having known Felicia all of her life, this book shows how determination and dedication can help you overcome many obstacles and challenges life throws at you. Felicia was destined for greatness, even as a child. I knew anything she wanted in life, she would, along with God's help, make it happen and that's exactly what she's done with her book entitled, "*Make It Happen, Moving Towards Your Best U!*" All readers, no matter what their background is, should definitely read this book. "We all face challenges and this book gives you touching and personal solutions in dealing with those challenges."

-Cheryl S. Tafoya, Executive Director
Keep Greenville Beautiful

"Do you long for a love like no other? Do you long for intimacy in that love relationship? If so, this is the book for you! I am moved by Felicia's honesty and transparency to share her real life experiences. As a daughter of the King, sister in Christ, wife, mother, manager in retail, she explains the real side of life and the importance of being connected to the love of our soul – Jesus Christ. The stories of her life are real and her advice is wise as she shares the awesome testimony of the Lord guiding her through her marriage, mothering, and career in good and difficult times. I pray reading this book will draw you into an intimate relationship with Jesus and let Him fill that empty hole in your heart that only He can fill. I also pray this book gives you the courage to read, believe and act on the truths in His Holy Word and by doing so, be transformed into the person God created you to be."

-Barnanne Creech – daughter of the King, wife of Rodney for 24 years, mom of 2 teens - Wade and Whitley, and middle school teacher

Published by His Glory Creations, Wendell, North Carolina

Copyright © 2016 by Felicia C. Lucas

ALL RIGHTS RESERVED

No portion of this publication may be reproduced, stored in any electronic system, or transmitted in any form or by any means, electronic, mechanical, photocopy, recording, or otherwise, without written permission from the author. Brief quotations may be used in literary reviews. Unauthorized reproduction of any part of this work is illegal and is punishable by law.

Scriptures are taken from the Holy Bible, New International Version®, NIV® unless otherwise noted. Copyright © 1973, 1978, 1984, 2011 by Biblica, Inc.™ Used by permission of Zondervan. All rights reserved worldwide. The "NIV" and "New International Version" are trademarks registered in the United States Patent and Trademark Office by Biblica, Inc.™

The Holy Bible, King James Version (KJV). Cambridge Edition: 1769; King James Bible Online, 2016. www.kingjamesbibleonline.org.

FOR INFORMATION CONTACT:

Felicia C. Lucas, "The Polishing Enthusiast"
Minister, Inspirational Speaker and Empowerment Coach
Online ordering is available for all products at www.felicialucas.com

ISBN-13: 978-0-692-70633-6

ISBN-10: 0-692-70633-0

Library of Congress Control Number: 2016908415

Because of the dynamic nature of the Internet, any web addresses referenced or links contained in this book may have changed since publication and may no longer be valid.

Stock imagery courtesy of Pixabay.com

Printed in the United States of America
10 9 8 7 6 5 4 3 2 1

TABLE OF CONTENTS

DEDICATION xi
ACKNOWLEDGEMENTS xiii
FOREWORD xv
PREFACE xvii

Chapter 1   The Intimacy Invitation 1
Chapter 2   Cultivate Your Love Relationship 11
Chapter 3   The K.I.S.S. Plan.. 22

Chapter 4   R U Maximizing? 32
Chapter 5   The Big C.H.O.P. 43
Chapter 6   Become a Person on the Move 52

Chapter 7   This is how you DO IT in the workplace 68
Chapter 8   Delayed but not Denied 80
Chapter 9   Moving towards WHOLENESS 90

AFTERWORD 108
ABOUT THE AUTHOR 112

DEDICATION

To my Lord and Savior, Jesus Christ, in you I live, move and have my being. I am nothing without you!

To my husband of 19½ years, Kelvin, thanks for being my best friend, my biggest supporter and partner in ministry. Thanks for all that you do behind the scenes to help me become my best! I know that you are my soul mate. I love you deeply!

To my children, Isaiah, Kelsey and Silas, I am proud of who you are becoming! Always keep God first in all that you do! You are destined for greatness!

To my parents, Ernest and Jo-Anne Clemons, sister, family members, in-laws and friends, thanks for your prayers!

A special dedication to the Matriarch of our family, my grandmother Clydie Mae Smith. Thanks for being a woman of faith!

To Cheryl Tafoya, thanks for all of your support during this book process!

To my friend for over 25 years, Denise Suggs Horne, you have been a tremendous blessing to me! I don't take you or our friendship for granted! I have always admired your love for God!

This book is dedicated to all those out there, who have ever struggled with their weight, have been rejected by others or felt like you had nothing to offer to the world. I hope my story inspires you to Make It Happen by Moving Towards your Best U!

ACKNOWLEDGEMENTS

Thank you Cherri Watson for the connection to the book midwife, Catrice M. Jackson. You both are phenomenal women that I am blessed to know! Thank you for your encouragement and support during this process! Catrice, I have learned so much from you during this journey. From the bottom of my heart, I am truly thankful for everything. Thanks for helping me to push out this baby!

A special thank you to the following individuals that assisted me with this project. I would not have been able to complete it, without your guidance and expertise:
Editor: Renee Dabney, The Write Bud
Interior Design and Formatting: Purposely Created Publishing
Photography and Cover Design: Kingdom Order Consulting

"For I know the plans I have for you, declares the Lord, plans to prosper you and not to harm you, plans to give you hope and a future." -Jeremiah 29: 11

Foreword

by Cherri Walston

I remember meeting Felicia for the first time at a conference for business and professional women. Our spirits connected, and we discovered that we both had a passion for helping others personally and professionally reach their highest potential. I was so excited to meet another kindred spirit who was passionate about serving, inspiring and empowering individuals to live their best YOU! This book embodies the tools, strategies and encouragement to do just that in a very transparent way. Felicia's gifts and life experiences supports every aspect of the reader's journey in discovering their purpose and goals for being their best selves. Her life, Christian walk, marriage, personal and professional journey is a guidepost for every young adult trying to figure it all out by themselves.

I love how the book starts out with developing an intimate relationship with God. Intimacy with the one who created you is the key to understanding who you are and what your purpose is in life. In my young adult years, I struggled with trying to figure out who I was, my purpose and what I wanted for my life. I was distracted by other's opinions of me and not truly understanding my own authenticity and divine natural abilities. I felt trapped. I didn't understand that intimacy with myself and with God was the glue that would seal the cracks in my life. It was later in life (after many challenges and mistakes) that I realized God had a plan for my life. I've learned that true intimacy with God and vital relationships are important to your spiritual growth and for maintaining healthy relationships.

Felicia eloquently states that intimacy is an invitation and like any invite it is your timely response, openness for connecting and affirming your presence for the gift of what's waiting for you in the present moment. The chapters in this simple, yet **Real Deal Talk**, is an invitation for you to live and be the best person you were created to be.

How can you make the things happen that you desire for your life, and the life you were designed to live? **Goals.** If you want to **Make It Happen**, you have to move with confidence in yourself and not by the perception of what other people might think. I coach and mentor individuals on living their vision, and I know firsthand that the way to make a transformation to your desired state is to take action. That action will require you walk in faith every day. Movement creates momentum and momentum produces the fruit you want to harvest in every aspect of your life. Felicia outlines every day issues, challenges, life events and general living with a teachable approach to Moving Towards your Best U! Her biblical principles, life applications and transparency makes it relatable for the young and seasoned individuals, who want more than just cookie-cutter anecdotes, but some **Real Deal Talk**. In today's world, we need more books that show you how to live your life by divine design to fulfill your greatness and **Make It Happen** is an example of how to elevate, take control and enter into your divine right for your highest good.

This book is a gift to every reader who desires to be inspired and empowered to be a trailblazer in their own life, with practical tools to maximize the power of SELF. It is an invitation awaiting your response of YES, to be the best you, you have ever seen. I hope you receive more than you can ever imagine or dream of. Cheers to making it happen!

—Cherri Walston, The BIG Vision Mentor for Women
Inspirational Speaker, Author, Visionary Entrepreneur –
Big Vision Biz, LLC
www.bigvisionmentor.com

PREFACE

"I find the great thing in this world is not so much where we stand, as in what direction we are moving - we must sail sometimes with the wind and sometimes against it - but we must sail, and not drift, nor lie at anchor." -Oliver Wendell Holmes Sr.

I almost did not write my story. Over three years ago, one of my sisters in Christ, Prophet Eartha Butler, suggested that I write a book, to share my personal, physical and professional successes with others. In my mind, I was saying...Who me? What do I have to share with the world? I really didn't believe initially I could do it. At first, I thought when I completed all of my life goals, then I would write the book. My decision to delay in sharing my story to the world was representative of me lying at anchor. I have experienced a lot in life, which makes up who I have become today. The book process accelerated when I decided to move from thinking, "I can't do this" to "Yes, I can do this!" I was able to put onto paper my life experiences in order to inspire others.

When you look at the process of making something happen, it means you cause something to exist or to come about. It requires action! I have learned when I do my part, God steps in and does his part, and I am able to continue towards my goals. God is looking for inspired individuals who are willing to engage themselves in the process and make things happen.

When you engage yourself, it involves effort on your part. Engagement can produce some perspiration, as a result of your effort. As humans, we perspire when we are engaged in intense constant motion. Perspiration comes when you put forth an effort to make things happen in your life. Many people desire the end results, but don't put forth the effort to obtain it! A good example of movement is found within the birth process.

As a mother of three children, I can certainly identify with the birth process. Just as babies are conceived, the ultimate goal is for them to eventually be born into the world. I remember being pregnant and experiencing the ups and downs of pregnancy. Some days were better than others, and like most mothers, I anxiously anticipated each of their arrivals. I experienced a difficult delivery with one of my children. I had a complication that caused my physician to use forceps. Forceps are a surgical instrument that resembles a pair of tongs. The tongs were used to help guide the baby out of my birth canal. My labor wasn't progressing and my baby's safety depended on an immediate delivery. This was an extremely painful part of the process. I endured this experience and thanks be unto God, my child was born without serious injuries.

Similarly, the birthing of this book was a process of excitement, anxiety, fear and fulfilment. I was excited about what the future could possibly hold, felt anxiety about making sure what I desired was captured in each chapter, had a little fear of the unknown and experienced fulfillment that I finally completed the project. A little discomfort here and there was pushing me towards this finished product.

At one point within the birthing process of this book, I experienced a complication that could have easily turned into a major setback. I spent some time on a particular day sharing with my husband some aspects of the book, more specifically the chapters on marriage. Little did we know, later that day, we would be faced with an attack against the very institution of our marriage. The attack caused tremendous pain at the moment, but I felt God was saying, "Just keep moving." Even the after effects of the words and actions of the attack are still disheartening. I would rehearse in my mind the words that were spoken over me and my marriage in the attack. I had to keep writing beyond my hurts and pain. I forgave the individual because it was necessary for me to move beyond that incident. What the devil meant for evil, God used for my good, and, as a result, the attack was further confirmation of the importance of sharing my story to the world! I celebrate God's faithfulness unto me as he has given me the grace to complete this assignment! Life is a process which includes successes, failures, ups, downs, disappointments and celebrations.

This book has been designed as an easy read with a workbook format. You will have the opportunity to record your thoughts and reflections as you work through the chapters. Please note the **Real Deal Talk** section at the end of each chapter. These talks allow me to be a little more candid and transparent about the subject matter at hand. I pray that my life experiences will inspire you to:

Make It Happen: Moving Towards Your Best U! Spiritually, Physically, Emotionally and Professionally

Chapter 1
The Intimacy Invitation

"You can KNOW about God and not KNOW God. The only way to know God is by doing LIFE with God and be a participator with him" -Joyce Meyer

Imagine going to your mailbox and finding a crumbled up envelope addressed to you, from a person that you know. They are inviting you to a special event in the near future. Not only is the envelope in bad shape, but you begin to look at the invitation and there are numerous misspelled words, the printing is hard to read, and they failed to include the time of the event. Would you become excited about attending their event?

Now imagine going to your mailbox and finding an envelope that is clean and crisp, your name is beautifully written, where you can see that the calligrapher took time with the stroke of the pen to make sure each letter of your name is exquisitely written. As you begin to pull out the inner envelope, you notice the satin ribbon matches the raised embossed emblem on the invitation. Every detail is intentional including the color of the paper and type of paper used. You get excited and anticipate an awesome upcoming event!

Have you ever been invited to something? How did it make you feel? People are generally invited to birthday parties, weddings, dinners, baby showers, graduations, retirement parties and cook-outs. When a host invites people to their event, they generally expect a response. Not just any response, but a timely response, which is often called a RSVP - a French term "répondez, s'il vous plait," which means "please reply." An invitation is requesting your presence or participation. Similarly, a marriage proposal is a type of invitation.

When a man invites a woman to be his wife, he proposes to her. Some proposals are very elaborate while others are quite simplistic. The proposal is an invitation for her to marry him. At this point, the woman has two options, to either accept or reject his invitation. The man's proposal for marriage is generally that they become joined together for the purpose of starting and maintaining a family. He should be proposing for her love, devotion and commitment for life. Upon accepting his marriage proposal, she is entering into a mutual relationship that is inclusive of endless devotion and commitment, which becomes the catalyst for her roles as wife and mother.

MY INTIMATE LOVE STORY

Kelvin and I met in April 1995, during a job interview in Atlanta, Georgia. We often joke about when we were on the plane, traveling from Raleigh to Atlanta, that he was sitting in the seat in front of me reading his itinerary, and I was curiously looking over his shoulder, and, by the time we landed, I knew he was a senior at North Carolina State University and that we were interviewing for the same job. He noticed my curiosity (*nosiness as he calls it*) and approached me as we were leaving the terminal to formally introduce himself. As we began to talk, we discovered that one of my college classmates from The University of North Carolina at Chapel Hill was also his cousin. We also knew three other people in common from his hometown. After a little chit-chat, we both went to our respective interviews, and I remember thinking that was most likely the last time I would see him. He seemed like a very nice guy, who had a good head on his shoulders and was also kind of cute.

One month later, I accepted the job offer and traveled down to Charlotte, North Carolina to begin my training. I was scheduled to be there for six weeks. I was a little nervous being in that big city, not knowing anyone. The next morning when I reported to the job site, Kelvin was in my training class. He had gotten the job as well! We instantly hit it off. He asked me out to dinners, the movies, to play mini-golf, the local theme park, and also to worship with him at a local church. I had never worshipped at church with a male companion. I felt very comfortable being with him. I was really enjoying his company!

After six weeks of training, I was assigned to technical training in Cary, North Carolina. Kelvin received his assignment for Raleigh, North Carolina, only fifteen minutes from me. I was happy and excited about being in this new relationship. I really liked that he was saved and loved God. Later in our relationship, Kelvin told me that before he went down to Charlotte, he asked God to direct his paths so he could meet a young lady, and it happened to be me, and I am so glad it was!

For the next six weeks, we continued to date while waiting to report to our assignments following technical training. He was assigned to Rocky Mount, North Carolina and my assignment was in Goldsboro, North Carolina, still within an hour drive of each other. We still maintained our relationship with frequent visits between our residences. No one at our jobs knew we were dating. When we did cross paths, we acted very professional.

Our friendship and relationship blossomed, and I was deeply head over heels for him. I was caught by surprise when he came to visit me on Wednesday the 27th of December, 1995. I remember the day as if it was yesterday, but it has been over twenty years ago. He asked me to marry him, and, of course, I said "yes." We didn't know what the future held, but we knew God had orchestrated our paths to cross.

We were engaged for a little over a year and were married February 15, 1997. We stood before God on that day and exchange these vows: Will you take Kelvin/Felicia to be your husband/wife, will you commit yourself to his/her happiness and his/her self-fulfillment as a person, and to his/her usefulness in God's kingdom, and will you promise to love, honor, trust and serve him/her in sickness and in health, in adversity and prosperity and to be true and loyal to him/her, so long as you both shall live? We were two souls uniting as one, passionately pursuing God's will for our lives. It wasn't about us; it was all about doing God's will.

We had no idea of the celebrations, triumphs and disappointments that life would bring: from accepting the call of being in ministry, to later founding a church and Non-profit Youth and Young Adult organization, and bouncing back financially from two layoffs, becoming the parents of three children, surviving the after effects of a miscarriage, to experiencing grief from the loss of several close loved ones, to purchasing and renovating our home and being able to travel. When I accepted his invitation, I did not know all of the challenges and successes that we would experience as a couple.

In comparison, just as a man proposes to a woman, God also proposes to mankind. He doesn't get down on one knee, but he gave his Son as the ultimate sacrifice for all that are willing to accept Him! God is a real gentleman. He does not force himself on anyone. ***In Revelation 3:20 (KJV), Jesus states: Behold I stand at the door and knock, if any man hears my voice and opens the***

door, I will come unto him and sup with him and he with me. You have the option to either accept or reject him. He is knocking at the door of your heart and wants you to be married to him, to have love, devotion and a lifetime of commitment. Prayer is the invitation for intimacy with God! He wants you to be in a committed relationship by having a prayer relationship with him. In the next chapter, I will provide tips on how to cultivate a prayer relationship with God.

What is the most popular form of intimacy that people think of in a marital relationship? Sex usually comes to mind. In a marriage, sex is very important but not the most important form of intimacy. Intimacy can be described as a close or loving personal relationship. God is concerned about the many things that may concern you, your relationships, friendships, home life and your job. ***The word says in 1 Peter 5:7, Cast all your anxiety on him, because he cares for you.***

One thing I have discovered about intimacy, especially in a marital relationship, is that intimacy is a process. It takes place over time and should not become stagnant. Stagnant relationships are relationships that have stopped developing, progressing or moving. Couples must be moving TOGETHER in the same direction forward, and not allow anything to impede their growth. About six years ago, we had reached a place in our marriage where our relationship was moving in the wrong direction. I was focused and determined to be an Entrepreneur, when I began my business, as an Independent Avon Representative. I had used Avon products before and knew the company was very established. My original plan was to have the business as a way to bring in extra income to our household budget, but soon discovered there were lucrative opportunities available, if I expanded my business.

My business blossomed and I went from an Independent Sales Representative to a Sales Unit Leader within eight months. Being a Sales Unit Leader of approximately fifty-five other Independent Sales Representatives was a major undertaking. Not only was I working a full-time job, but I was running this business on the side, which meant that on my days off, when I was scheduled late for my full-time job or on the afternoons when I left from my full time job, I was doing the Avon business. Subsequently, I had Avon meetings and gatherings on Thursdays, which is also the night in which our church meets for Bible study, so I started missing church as well. So the First Lady of the church was building her Avon business, but losing her husband and family in the process. I had no clue what was going on with my kids at school because I was never home. My kids needed their mother; my husband needed his wife and where was I? So of course, it started to affect my marriage. I was not spending time creating intimacy with him, but I was looking at the money and not looking at the big picture as to what it was costing me: my husband and my children. I was not moving towards my best me! I was growing farther-and-farther away from being in balance and in control of my life!

I remember driving to work one morning and receiving a call from my husband who flat out asked me did I want to be a part of this family, did I really want to be married, or did I just want to do my own thing? For me, that was a major wake up call; this side gig could cost me my family, and I immediately made a decision right then that the extra money was really not worth it if I would be spending it, all alone, by myself. So I called my leader that morning and told her that I would not be able to continue in that capacity with Avon, and I have not looked back since! Yes, I still sell Avon but it is on my own terms, and I determine how much time I wish to devote to it. Since my husband and I started to rebuild our intimacy and strengthened our relationship, we can now say that our relationship continues to be progressive.

STAGNATION KILLS INTIMACY!

Good relationships don't just happen; they take time and patience and two people who truly want to be together. Your prayer relationship with God takes time to grow and develop as well. Your prayer relationship must be progressive.

In **Luke 10:38-42**, the Bible tells the story of Jesus and his disciples visiting friends of Jesus named Mary and Martha. These women were sisters of Lazarus, who was raised from the dead by Jesus. Because of the close relationship that Jesus had with these women, I know they were so excited about having him in their home. Just think, if Jesus was coming to pay you a visit, you would want to make sure that he has an awesome experience. **Luke 10:39**, deals with the fact that Mary decided to sit at Jesus's feet to receive wisdom from him. Our prayer relationship gives us an opportunity to spend time in his presence. One interesting fact that draws much attention is these two women had different responses to the presence of Jesus in their home. In **Luke 10:40**, it describes Martha as being distracted and cumbered. When someone is cumbered, they are troubled or burdensome. So what would cause these two women to have two different responses to his visit? Martha was more concerned about the act of preparing the food and the atmosphere of the home, and Mary was focused on drawing closer to Christ, by sitting at his feet, in his presence, hearing God's word. Mary had a desire to have an intimate encounter with Christ.

In modern times, you can't physically sit at his feet, but you can get in his presence with your prayer relationship! You must desire him in all that you say and do. You can't get so caught up in doing things in life that you miss the intimate time spent with God. Martha missed the real reason why Jesus came to visit in the first place. She even interrupted his teaching to ask him why Mary was not helping her fix the food. Martha was a little stressed about his visit, and, when Mary chose to sit at his feet, it really exposed the anxiety that Martha was experiencing. Martha failed to see that being in Jesus's presence was very important. Jesus used this time in **Luke 10: 41-42** to tell Martha what her problem was. She was so troubled about many things, but what was the condition of her heart towards him? Mary made a conscious decision to follow after Jesus, which was very much needed. He was needed then and he is needed now! Can you relate to Martha? Are you substituting things, other people, your job, organizations that you belong to instead of choosing to have an intimate relationship with God?

Your heart's desire should be like the deer *in **Psalm 42:1** which reads: As the deer pants for streams of water, so my soul pants for you, my God!* The deer looks until it finds water to quench its' thirst. In comparison, you should look until you find the living water, which is Jesus Christ, so your brook will never go dry again. Your heart should yearn and desire to deepen your prayer relationship with him, so you can receive the insight on how to fulfill your assignment here on earth. All assignments are different, but your ultimate goal should be to please the Father. Mary made the choice to sit at Jesus's feet, which shows her devotion to Christ. She knew there was a time and a season for business, and she recognized the food could wait. She made a choice to have Christ as a priority and nothing could take the place of spending time in his presence.

A priority is something that is regarded as more important than something else. When something is a priority, it is at the top of the list of what is going on. **Who or what is your number #1 Priority?**

Mary was making an eternal investment by choosing this time with Jesus. What eternal investments are you making in your life?

_____

_____

Is intimacy with God a priority? Why or why not?

_____

_____

He truly desires a close and loving relationship with all who are willing to let him into their hearts.

Step 1: Make It Happen: Moving Towards Your Best U!

Have you accepted God's Intimacy Invitation today? If not, are you willing to? Why or why not?

_____

_____

REAL DEAL TALK

If you are single and can't identify with my love story, your challenge is to create your own intimacy love story with God as a single individual. Just as the husband has the capacity to impregnate his wife, so that she can produce children, God desires to impregnate you with his wisdom, knowledge and understanding, so that you can **Move Towards your Best U!** *As your Best U, you will become empowered to share your gifts, talents and ideas with the world!*

Now in reference to my intimate love story: I would not have given Kelvin a second look if he had presented himself to me like the crumbled up envelope - someone who has no pride in themselves, no level of confidence, or not trying to go far in life. Kelvin was well mannered, dressed nicely and his conversation was not about a bunch of foolishness. No one is perfect by any means, but a potential mate should be moving towards being a positive asset in your life and not a liability. You can consider an intimacy invitation with a person who is compatible with where you are going in life and displays qualities such as: godliness, ambition and confidence.

Chapter 2
Cultivate your Love Relationship

"That is why a man leaves his father and mother and is united to his wife, and they become one flesh. " Genesis 2:24

A relationship with God is the most important relationship you can have. Even though my relationship with my husband is the most important natural relationship that I have, my relationship with God is my priority. I know my life means nothing without having his guidance each and every day. As a child of God, you must learn to embrace your relationship with God every day!

I like to use the relationship comparison to what a farmer does in order to get the results they want. If the farmer plants apple seeds, then the expectation is that an apple tree will manifest itself at the end of the process. **Cultivation is a key component in yielding fruit.** To cultivate means to develop, grow, become more mature and advance. An apple seed which does not grow will always be just a seed. The goal is for it to become an apple tree. The process of cultivation is never easy. It takes hard work and sacrifice. Sometimes the farmer has to rise early or work late to get the results they desire. A farmer can lose money if their seeds don't yield fruit at harvest time. Fruit comes when the farmer makes things happen and engages themselves in the process, by not just planting the seed but also by fertilizing and pruning. When the seed grows, the end product, is very different from what it looked like in the beginning, and the farmer realizes that all the blood, sweat and tears are well worth the wait.

In comparison, it is very important that you cultivate your relationship with God through Jesus Christ daily. You must make an investment for it to become more mature. **In Peter 1:8**, Peter recognizes his audience for loving and believing in Christ, even though they had not physically seen him. Love and faith are the two most important ingredients needed for a successful relationship with God. Just as the farmer plants the seed, by reading this book you are planting a seed of **FAITH,** and you are responsible for cultivating that seed. The cultivating process starts with **PLANTING,** which consists of but is not limited to the following components:

> *Daily Prayer Time with God*
> *Reading and Studying God's Word*
> *Daily Devotionals*
> *Be a member of an Early Riser's Ministry or Prayer Group*

DAILY PRAYER TIME WITH GOD

Prayer time with God will look different for each of you. The length and frequency is not what is most important. Prayer is the most essential way to cultivate an intimacy relationship with God. I used to think that prayer was about being "deep and spiritual," praying for endless hours and speaking in tongues continuously, but what I have come to know is that prayer is just having simple conversations with God. You can't get any plainer than that. Talking with God should be like it is when you talk with a friend or love one. You are very open, honest and express exactly what is on your heart and mind.

Your conversations with him can be that real and honest. What types of conversations do you need to have with him? There are several prayer conversations that you can use:

>**PRAYERS OF INTERCESSION:** *Praying to God about others*
>
>**PRAYERS OF CELEBRATION:** *Honoring God for who he is*
>
>**PRAYERS OF GRATITUDE:** *Thanking God for what he has done*
>
>**PRAYERS OF ACKNOWLEDGMENT:** *Talking to God about your sins and asking for forgiveness*
>
>**PRAYERS OF PETITION:** *Asking God for self-help*
>
>**PRAYERS OF DEVOTION:** *Expressing to God that you will do what he desires for you to do*
>
>**PRAYERS OF FAVOR:** *Asking for God's Blessing*

Incorporating these prayers into your daily life will be life changing. I encourage you to use as many of the above ways to help cultivate your own prayer life. In order to grow and mature in your relationship with God, you must have these types of prayer conversations.

READ AND STUDY GOD'S WORD

With all the technology that is available in the world, there are so many devices that can be used to read the Bible. When I travel, I can open the dresser drawer in my hotel room and find a copy of the Gideon's Bible. The Bible is also available on CD, audio tapes, MP3's and podcasts. There are also many versions of the Bible available. The most common is the King James Version (KJV). I personally find the New International Version (NIV) easier to understand and read, especially when I study. The NIV Bible captures a simpler version of the original biblical text (KJV) that you can use to apply to your life.

Other useful resources are the Concordance, Bible dictionary, and a Webster's dictionary. Bible dictionaries share the historical and cultural importance of the text. The Concordance is an alphabetical index of the principal words of the Bible, with a reference to the passage in which each occurs. This is great when you need to find a particular scripture and to see where that reference occurs in other books of the Bible. A Webster's dictionary is also very useful to define what a word means, which determines what the author is trying to convey to the audience. Studying the books of the Bible is far more than just flipping through the chapters and reading the words. It's about asking yourself the question who was that particular book written to and why was it written? Studying the Bible will also give you a chance to find where you can relate to a particular character and see the results in their life and how God was a part of it. This is how the Bible becomes applicable to a person's life when they can find themselves within the text.

DAILY DEVOTIONALS

There are several paperback booklets which can be mailed to the reader each month for a nominal fee. The method that I personally prefer is the electronic versions, which are delivered to my email or my Facebook feed each morning. The following are some daily devotionals booklets that are also available on-line: The Daily Bread and The Upper Room. You can also program your phone to send you text messages periodically throughout the day with inspirational verses and messages.

BE A PART OF AN EARLY RISER'S PRAYER MINISTRY OR PRAYER GROUP

When one of my friends invited me to dial into an Early Riser's Prayer Group, I immediately thought it would be a struggle to do so because of my varying work schedule. I called in one morning and have been calling in since for the past two years. The Early Riser's Morning Prayer Group meets each morning, Monday-Friday at 5:30 am, for approximately 30 minutes. This time is used for prayer requests, words of encouragement and praise reports. I have even had the opportunity to share an encouraging and inspirational message with the group as part of our Thank God it's Friday (TGIF) sessions. This prayer group has enhanced my personal relationship with God and connected me with other believers across the United States. Implementing simple steps such as the previous ones discussed can help you enjoy a more fulfilled and enjoyable relationship with God.

Likewise, cultivating a marital relationship is very similar to our prayer relationship with God. My husband and I have implemented the list below to cultivate our marriage:

Spending time together

Couple's Devotionals

Praying Together

Date Night, Date Days and Excursions

SPENDING TIME TOGETHER

The first thing a lot of people think of when you say that couples spend time together is in a sexual way. I beg to differ; there are other things that you can do besides engaging in sexual activity. I would really re-evaluate one's marital relationship if it is only about sex. For our relationship, the foundation had to be about God and based on friendship. As couples get older, a physical change occurs, so sexual attraction can't be the only thing keeping a couple together. Don't get me wrong; sex is important, and, for us, some of our other priorities are expressive interactions such as, morning walks at our local park, playing games of Scrabble and watching episodes of old shows such as: The Love Boat, The Jefferson's, Good Times and Sanford & Son.

Just like you put important appointments on your electronic calendar or day planner, your date times need to be included as well. Blocking out the time shows your commitment to your spouse and the seriousness of the time set aside for the date. My husband also writes our dates on our family calendar, so everyone in the household is well informed about the plans for that particular date.

My husband and I alternate what kind of things we do during our date times. It would not be fun if the activity chosen brought pleasure to only one individual on the date. We both love sports, so going to a College Football/Basketball Game or attending a NBA Basketball Game would be considered a mutual activity for us. Choosing different activities for each date keeps things interesting and not boring. Trying new activities is also a way to discover new interests which may become a new favorite. Dates should be designed to create intimacy, which leads to an individual becoming their best in reference to their marital relationship. **Our time is our time, and we don't take it for granted!**

COUPLE'S DEVOTIONALS

We received Moments Together for Couples by Dennis and Barbara Rainey as one of our wedding gifts. This devotional contains daily scriptures along with a real life story related to the Bible where couples can read together. Each reading is listed by date, to help you stay on track. There are discussion starters and prayers at the end of each reading to help get you talking about the topic for that day.

Here is an example from their book: January 12

Discuss: Why do you marry? What did you hope to get out of the marriage?

Pray: That God will spare you and your family from drifting aimlessly through life and that He will give your family His purpose, plan and direction.

I also subscribe weekly to emails by ministries with a focus on marital subjects and weekly marriage devotionals, such as Marriage Today by Jimmy Evans. Here are some excerpts from a recent email: "*Marriage is a covenant. In the Bible, the word covenant means «to cut.» You don't make a covenant, you cut a covenant. Every time a covenant appears in the Bible, blood is involved. Jesus said, "This is my blood of the covenant, which is poured out for many for the forgiveness of sins" (Matthew 26:28). That means sacrifice is central to the idea of a covenant. It is a sacrificial, permanent relationship. The wedding vows we take are covenant vows. When we say, "for better or worse, for richer or poorer, in sickness and in health," we are stating the vows of a sacrificial covenant relationship...Marriage is a sacrifice. It's hard work. It's a sacrificial covenant vow that says, "During good times and bad, I'm all in. It may not be a walk in the park, but it's worth it. I'm dedicated to serving you. I'm dedicated to* making our marriage work." That covenant mindset is the secret to a lasting marriage." **Blessings, Jimmy Evans**

I also read several Facebook marriage inspirational pages, which fill my news feeds with marital subjects that my husband and I often discuss.

One of my favorite marriage Facebook pages is: Marriage Works! Healthy Marriages, Functional Families.

PRAYING TOGETHER

There is nothing like taking your spouse by the hand and going forth together in a word of prayer. There is so much power when both are on one accord with God. My husband and I pray together as a couple as often as we can. And, just as important is the need for us to PRAY FOR EACH OTHER. I pray that God's will be done for our lives and that God continues to provide revelations to us as a couple. If you are married, no one should be praying more for your spouse than you.

DATE NIGHT, DATE DAYS AND WEEKEND GET-A-WAYS

The intimacy within our marriage accelerated when we started having date nights, date days and various weekend get-a-ways. When we moved outside of traditional thinking of what a date should look like, we saw the extreme importance of doing them. In the past, we would only celebrate our Wedding Anniversary and Birthdays. As parents, we now understand that we need a break from our kids, and our kids need a break from us! We are very blessed to have people in our lives who are willing to babysit, so we can go on our adventures.

It is not uncommon for us to go out for the evening, to dinner and a movie, and then retreat to a hotel room for the night. We often stay at hotels in the Raleigh area, even though we live about thirty minutes away from our date sites. It is so heavenly to wake up to a completely quiet atmosphere where one can just enjoy the company of each other. We always try to explore many areas of intimacy during this time. We have to become a little creative when the kids are in school, so we created Date Days, by catching a movie matinee, walking around the mall or grabbing lunch. All these times are designed for us to cultivate our love relationship.

We both have discovered that we love to travel. It feels great to get out of the state of North Carolina and go to places we have never been. God has blessed us tremendously over the past few years that we have had the opportunity to travel to some exciting destinations near and far on the East and West Coast, out of the country, and in the Caribbean. I am not sharing to boast or to brag. I share so that you can be inspired to save your money, plan your trips and enjoy a similar experience. We really have a blast at our travel destinations and create memories that we will sit on our front porch, as we get older, and reminisce about. It only happened when we made it happen. It takes effort on our part to have the money to travel and plan exciting things to do during our get-a-ways. To see the world, with our own eyes, has been something that we don't take for granted! I am thankful that we have the opportunity to cultivate our love relationship in this way!

Step 2: Make It Happen: Moving Towards Your Best U!

What do you need to do to cultivate your relationship with God?

_____
_____
_____
_____

How can you cultivate a relationship with your spouse?

_____
_____
_____
_____

What needs to change or to be added to your current life?

_____
_____
_____
_____

REAL DEAL TALK

There have been times when we had no clue as to how we would be able to fund our get-a-ways. My husband is a planner, so he is looking a year out, which gives us the chance to save money and have a plan in place to reach our goal. For our Nineteenth Wedding Anniversary, he secured our baby sitter and made plans about what we were going to do on the trip. We saved up the necessary funds for the trip and then…. life happened, some unexpected expenses occurred that caused us to spend the money we set aside for the trip. My husband and I were disappointed, but he continued to plan the trip as if we were still going. Three days before we were scheduled to leave, yes three days, we received a financial blessing that covered all of the expenses for the trip! He purchased our plane tickets, secured our hotel reservations and all of the other items needed for the trip in that short window of time! Everything was paid for, we went on our trip, had a great time, and, looking back, we have no regrets! **God's favor is AWESOME!**

Chapter 3
The K.I.S.S. PLAN

"Commit to the LORD WHATEVER YOU DO, and he will establish your plans." Proverbs 16:3

Whenever I deliver the K.I.S.S. message during one of my relationship seminars, the married couples start to sit a little taller and move to the edge of their seats. The single people give me a look that says, "I know she is not getting ready to talk to us about kissing!" I just continue on with my discussion, and soon they all are exposed to what I mean by the K.I.S.S. plan! The K.I.S.S. plan stands for: **Keep It So Simple!** Plans that are simple and easy to follow will increase your probability of success. Sometimes the less steps you have within the plan, the greater the probability of achieving your desired outcome. It is possible to go farther with fewer steps than you can with too many steps.

In order for things to happen as you would like for them to in life, a plan is necessary. A plan is simply an intentional roadmap towards a goal that you have established. When you do something intentionally, it is done on purpose, deliberately and fully calculated! Think about a time in your life when you did not have a plan to reach a goal. How did it turn out? Did you reach it or were you unsuccessful in achieving your desired outcome? Whenever a plan is involved, you can have two basic mindsets concerning the plan:

Mindset (A) Let It Happen   Mindset (B) Make It Happen

When individuals have a *Let it Happen Mindset*, there is no plan and no guide in reaching the goal. They settle for whatever ends up happening. It is when the popular slogan, "It is what it is" becomes the norm. Any area of your life including your goals, dreams, career, or relationships have the capacity to be successful when a plan is developed and put into action. However when you have a *Make it Happen Mindset,* you realize that when you *Make it Happen*, you have a plan, execute your plan, and you overcome any opposition against your plan. A plan that is done with purpose can yield the results that you seek. Plans can either be complex or simple.

Have you ever felt like there are never enough hours in the day to get done what you think needs to get done? Do you ever feel as though you are walking on a tight rope in life, always on edge, trying to get from point A to point Z? Have you ever been afraid that you would slip and fall off that tight rope and never reach your goals? I know what all of this feels like.

There was a time in my life in which I was really out of balance: Spiritually, Physically, Emotionally, Mentally and Professionally. I was trying to hold it all together, with too many steps, but I was not being very successful in doing so. I found myself doing a whole lot of stuff, but I was not living a simple plan. In actuality, I was making my life a whole lot more complex than what it needed to be. K.I.S.S. requires you to take an assessment of the many roles and responsibilities that you have and make a decision about what is actually important. What roles or responsibilities do you currently have?

_____

_____

_____

_____

_____

HERE ARE A FEW OF MINE

Woman	Entrepreneur
Wife	Full Time Employee (A Manager and Trainer)
Mother	Community Activist
First Lady	Friend
Minister	Other Family Roles
Author	

You have already learned that having a relationship with God should be the top priority in your life. The things you choose to do in life should cultivate that relationship and not hinder it. When you spend time focusing on things that have little or no relevance to your Godly purpose, you are wasting valuable time. The Bible states in **Mark 8:36 (KJV): *"For what shall it profit a man, to gain the whole world and to lose his own soul?"*** When you invest countless hours towards complex agendas which yield nothing, it often prevents you from developing that simple plan which could produce greatness. In developing your intimacy with God, I would like to offer you four SIMPLE steps:

1. *DECIDE THE BEST TIME TO HAVE YOUR ALONE TIME WITH GOD*
2. *FIND A PRIVATE PLACE WHERE YOU WILL NOT BE INTERRUPTED OR DISTRACTED*
3. *WRITE DOWN YOUR THOUGHTS, IDEAS AND PRAYERS SPOKEN AND HEARD DURING THIS TIME*
4. *OFFER THANKS UNTO GOD FOR THE OPPORTUNITY AND REPEAT STEPS ONE-FOUR THE NEXT DAY*

DECIDE THE BEST TIME TO HAVE YOUR ALONE TIME WITH GOD

This will be different for every individual. Some people prefer early in the morning while others choose right before they go to bed, and others carve out time within their day, which works best for them. Since I have a forty-minute commute to my full-time job, I often use this time. It depends on your preferences when you are able to become the most engaged with your interactions with God. For me, early morning time often works too because I am a morning person by nature. I feel most alive and alert at 5:00 am verses at 10:00 pm. **REMEMBER THE CHOSEN TIME IS NOT THE FOCUS. IT'S HAVING THE TIME WITH HIM THAT MATTERS THE MOST!** A quiet time with God is designed for renewal and to provide you with strength. If you make it a priority, then all of the other things in life will be so much more bearable.

FIND A PRIVATE PLACE WHERE YOU WILL NOT BE INTERRUPTED OR DISTRACTED

My family recently watched a movie entitled, "The War Room," where the major character developed her private space by using her existing closet in her home. Her space was free of all distractions, so she could fully focus on spending time with God. Not everyone has an extra closet to do this, so you have to make the most of the space you have. When I am at home, I spend the majority of my quiet time in my bedroom. During this time, the television is off, the cell phone is turned off, and the most important piece is that I am not interrupted. Where in your home or living space could you use for your private time? Is this area free of technological devices and people, so you can spend your quality time with God? If you don't have an identified space, what creative concept do you have to implement a proper place?

WRITE DOWN YOUR THOUGHTS, IDEAS AND PRAYERS SPOKEN AND HEARD DURING THIS TIME

Keeping a written record is a valuable way to document what you hear God say. Journaling will be a way for you to express your thoughts and desires. During this quiet time, you may get strategies, ideas and suggestions to move your life to the next level. Remember it is a two-way conversation; you speak to God, and God will speak back to you. He will also show you through his Word the answer to the prayers that you are offering up to him. Sometimes he is silent, and it may seem he is not listening. Rest assured that he is always listening, and, even when he does not respond, don't give up on him; he never gives up on you. He loves you and only wants the Best for your life! You can also use this time to declare affirmations over your life. When you speak affirmations, you are speaking with authority that something exists or is true. Even if it doesn't presently look like it now, still speak affirmations. Here are some affirmations to say during your quiet time with God:

I AM…..

God's Child	Healed	Beautiful	Generous
Loved	Forgiven	Fruitful	Grateful
Favored	Successful	Equipped	Motivated
Able	Empowered	Courageous	Inspired
Encouraged	Blessed	Unstoppable	Amazing
Confident	Victorious	Gifted	Original
Anointed	Healthy	Whole	Committed
Free	Winning	Happy	Talented

Speak these over your life instead of death. ***Proverbs 18:21 (KJV) states: "Death and life are in the power of the tongue"*** When those around you begin to speak negative things, come right back with, "No…..I am not who you say that I am. I am God's masterpiece and I am _____! "(Fill in the Blank with a word listed above).

OFFER THANKS UNTO GOD FOR THE OPPORTUNITY AND REPEAT STEPS ONE-FOUR THE NEXT DAY

Giving thanks unto God for the opportunity to be in his presence is an excellent expression of gratitude towards him. I know from being a parent of three children, when they show me sincere gratitude for the things that I do for them, I am more eager to do more for them. Well, God is the same way! The word says in ***Matthew 6:33, "But seek first his kingdom and his righteousness, and all these things will be given to you as well."*** When you *seek his way, will, desires and thank him for just being God*, he will give you exactly what you need to accomplish his purpose within you for that day. *He will be waiting for you to return on the next day. Will you show up?*

Take a moment and think about what personal goals you have in your life. It can be in the areas of your spiritual life, career, educational aspirations, relationships, financial or personal growth.

One Personal Goal you have is to _____

_____:

Put the action steps in order to obtain this goal:

1.

2.

3.

4.

EXAMPLE:

One Personal Goal that you may have is to <u>Go Back to School</u>

Put the action steps in order to obtain this goal:

1. Decide what you would like to study.

2. Go on-line and research potential schools.

3. Talk to other people currently doing what you want to do.

4. Explore financial aid options.

As you begin to formulate your plans, be mindful that your plan may not always go as you plan it to. When you implement your plan, you will face obstacles. Implementation requires action or movement. The key to success is if you can overcome those obstacles. Overcoming involves having success when dealing with a difficulty. Have you ever overcome in any areas of your life? If so, take a minute and jot down thoughts about what your process to overcome looked like:

_____

_____

_____

_____

_____

_____

Generally, when people have a plan in their mind, they can see the end result in the future. It is a straight shot from Point A to Point Z. Actually, the plan may end up looking a little like this: you may hit some hard places, have some bridges to cross, feel overwhelmed at times and feel like there is no sunshine. All of these can be seen as obstacles. An obstacle is anything that blocks a person's way or hinders progress. God will give you signs as you go along, such as:

The most important thing is to see the signs that he gives you.

EXAMPLE OF OBSTACLES WHICH KEEP YOU FROM COMPLETING YOUR PLAN

Mindset of the Individual: Thinking that you can't accomplish the plans that you have in place.

Not having enough time to do the plan: Having many other commitments that are occupying your time.

Other people: Sometimes you may allow other people's opinions of you to affect your plans.

What obstacles have you identified in your life?

_____

_____

_____

The key is to identify the obstacle and eliminate it, so you can continue with your plan. The ultimate plan is to take your plan from start to finish, implement it, overcome obstacles and reach the celebration stage. Reaching a goal and persevering through is commendable. Many people give up during the process and don't reach their maximum capacity. Keeping the plan simple will help in the process of obtaining the goal.

Step 3: Make It Happen: Moving Towards Your Best U! Practice the K.I.S.S.

How will you celebrate when you reach your goal?

_____

_____

REAL DEAL TALK

There are times that I don't feel like the affirmation words that I am speaking are helping me on that particular day. There are days that I am a little stressed or have a whole lot of stuff going on, that I don't even want to pray. I am so glad that God does not treat me like I sometimes treat him. He is always available and he continues to provide for me even when I don't deserve it. Sometimes I have to look myself in the mirror and say, "Girl, you are better than this. Get yourself together!" God, in his loving kindness, gives me the grace to persevere one more day!

Chapter 4

R U Maximizing?

"Your gifts don't always show up immediately. God uses your experiences to draw out of you skills and gifts you didn't even know you had!"
- Bishop T. D. Jakes

My earliest memory of working with young people was when I was asked to conduct youth hour at my home church, Corey's Chapel Free Will Baptist Church. The youth hour leader was the late Mother Cora P. Montgomery. She always encouraged me to participate in church activities. She was a retired educator by trade and displayed Godly grace to all that she came in contact with. Just being around this phenomenal woman of God was so inspiring. She would always ask me how I was doing in school, and I loved the fruit bags that she would give to all the children at church during Christmas.

Youth hour was on every third Sunday during the morning worship service. It was not an hour long, rather approximately ten to fifteen minutes of her giving us encouraging words. At the end of the session, each youth present had to recite or read a Bible verse. I always wanted to find the longest verse to recite during that time. Some of the others would chose the easiest Bible verse, like Jesus wept, as their verse. I was always excited about speaking my verse before the congregation. She always ended the youth hour with her prayer, "Accept our gratitude oh Lord, for all the blessings, thou giveth. Direct and guide our daily paths and teach us how to live, for Christ's sake, Amen"! I still remember those words, over thirty-eight years later. Those words were true then and they are still true now. When I got older, she asked me to be a speaker for the youth hour. I was so excited to do so! Her encouragement early in life catapulted my interest in talking in front of crowds of people.

What passions in life have you identified that excite you? Has someone ever told you that you are a "natural" at something? What is **that thing** that you can do with ease, practically with no effort on your part? That thing is what I call your ***BTDT***, Your Born to Do This! The sooner one taps into their ***BTDT***, the easier one's life will begin to move towards operating in Godly purpose. People sometimes recognize it way before you can recognize it. Once your ***BTDT*** self is recognized, how do you maximize your opportunities in the world?

YOUR BTDT IS: _____

When you begin to think about the word maximize, several things can come to mind. To maximize means to increase to full potential, to make the most of. When one says they have maximized something, it simply means they have obtained the greatest quantity or value attainable. Are you maximizing in the following areas of your life?

YOUR TIME

YOUR SPIRITUAL WALK

YOUR PHYSICAL HEALTH AND WELL-BEING

YOUR PROFESSIONS OR OCCUPATIONS

YOUR FINANCES

YOUR ABILITIES OR TALENTS

YOUR TIME

Time is the most important thing you have. How you chose to manage it can have a huge impact on your present and future. Who or what you consider as a priority can also shape and define the essence of who you are. The Bible says in **John 9:4,** *"**As long as it is day, we must do the works of him who sent me. Night is coming when no one can work."** This means while you have breath in your body, you must work and do that which you were born to do!

YOUR SPIRITUAL WALK

Are you studying, reading the word, and praying like you should? Are you reading inspirational passages or listening to uplifting music? Do you take advantage of spending daily quiet time with God?

YOUR PHYSICAL HEALTH AND WELL-BEING

Are you eating the right foods for your body? Do you drink water daily? Can you commit daily to walking or physical activity to promote heart healthiness? Do you go to your doctor for an annual physical exam? Do you follow the recommended checks in getting a pap smear, prostate exam, mammogram or colonoscopy?

YOUR PROFESSION OR OCCUPATION

Are you working in the right field or in the right job? Do you just show up every day or do you want to make a difference? I am a firm believer in **Colossians 3:23, which states, *"Whatever you do, work at it with all your heart, as working for the Lord, not for human masters."*** I believe this definitely applies to our jobs. Are you an ideal employee or are you a Human Resources nightmare? God wants you to honor him by being honorable, wherever you work in the marketplace.

YOUR FINANCES

This is an area in which a lot of families struggle. Over 50% of marriages that end in divorce cite money problems as a reason. Do you honor God in how you spend your money? Do you consult his guidance on major purchases or financial decisions? Does your household have a budget? Do you know how much your family spends a week on non-essential things? Do you save any of your income, or do you spend every dime of it? Do you know how to manually balance your checkbook?

YOUR ABILITIES OR TALENTS

There is a parable that is found in **Matthew 25**, which addresses how people should maximize. A parable is simply an earthly story about heavenly concepts. Jesus often spoke to the crowds of people with a natural and relatable story that the individual could identify with, and he would then connect it to a spiritual matter. Jesus was and is still very relevant to his audience.

The story begins with a few characters, a man and his servants. Servants are simply ones that serve or perform duties for a person or in a home environment. It is common that individuals with money, wealth, status or position, employ many servants to assist in various capacities. Many people don't like to take on the role of a servant. There are negative connotations associated in being a servant. In actuality, being a servant is the ultimate form of worship unto God. When you put the needs of others before yours, it shows unselfishness. The problem in many servant/master situations is when the master abuses their authority and takes advantage of the servant. A servant grins and bears things even if they don't feel like doing something. A master who treats their servant with respect, in return, will receive eternal loyalty from their servant.

The Bible states that he entrusted his wealth unto these servants. When one entrusts, they commit to another with confidence. Confidence that the servant would take care of the property or item as if it was their own. Have you ever loaned something to someone and they returned it to you damaged, broken, or not at all? I remember years back, I let one of my co-workers borrow a cassette tape of one of my favorite artists. They had it for a few weeks, and, when it was time for me to receive my tape back, they said, "Sorry, but your tape popped in my player." I was not happy with the end result. I did not have my favorite tape, and, to top it off, they didn't even volunteer to replace it. I had entrusted it to them, and my expectation was that I would get my tape back as it was given unto them.

In Matthew 25: 14-29, the master not only entrusted his wealth, but also his valuable possessions to his servants. One translation refers to wealth as being a talent. A talent was considered to be a very large sum of money. Talents for our purposes can be your abilities and gifts, and how you use them in the earth realm. Talents can be natural, acquired or spiritual.

- **NATURAL ABILITIES** are things that you are good at simply because of genetics. They are given by God through your parents at birth. Some examples of natural abilities include: Intelligence quotient (I.Q.), athletics, and musical strengths.

- **ACQUIRED ABILITIES** are learned abilities, which can include: cooking, sewing, learning to play an instrument and learning a foreign language.

- **SPIRITUAL GIFTS** are God given abilities for Christian service that are given by God, independent of your parents. These gifts are manifested through the power of the Holy Spirit and given to benefit the Body of Believers in Christ.

Here are some examples of spiritual gifts:

Administration	*Apostle*	*Craftsmanship*	*Discernment*
Encouragement	*Evangelism*	*Faith*	*Giving*
Healing	*Helping*	*Hospitality*	*Knowledge*
Interpretation of Tongues	*Leadership*	*Mercy*	*Miracles*
Missions	*Music*	*Pastoring*	*Prayer*
Prophesy	*Serving*	*Teaching*	*Tongues*
Wisdom			

If you are unsure of your spiritual gifts, there are several free on-line assessments that you can take. One quick survey is found at: http://www.umc.org/what-we-believe/spiritual-gifts-online-assessment

YOUR SPIRITUAL GIFTS ARE

_____

_____

_____

In the **Matthew 25** story, the Master gave out five talents to one servant, two talents to another and one talent to his other servant. As a recipient of five talents, the question could have been "Am I worthy?" As a recipient of one talent, "Is this all? Does the master care about me? Why did they receive more?" Have you ever compared your gifts to others? In response, the master gave each of them according to their abilities. One's ability is your capacity to handle something. How people maximize looks different to many people!

The servant with five talents moved quickly to put his talent to work, and, as a result, he gained five more talents. He doubled what he had. Do you have a sense of urgency to execute the things of God in the earth? ***Matthew 25:17*** states, the individual that had received two talents, gained two additional talents. In verse 18, the servant with one talent dug a hole and hid his talent in the ground. When you hide something, it is removed out of sight and becomes concealed. Sometimes people keep things a secret in hopes to evade responsibility. What are you avoiding or hiding that God has given unto you? What are you keeping a secret that could be shared to aid in someone else's break through?

_____

_____

_____

_____

_____

The story progresses in verse 19 with, after a passage of time. Time can often show you missed opportunities. What opportunities have come your way over time? What ideas have crossed your path or come through your hands? The KJV states, the master reckoned with his servants. When you reckon, it means to count or to compute. You can begin by looking at what you started with and view what you currently have. There is so much value in stopping and comparing where you were and where you are now.

THIS IS CALLED PROGRESS!

Has your thinking, ways of functioning and how you handle your life changed any over time? If so, how?

_____

_____

_____

_____

In your reflection, did you discover that you were better than you used to be? In verse 20, the servant which had five talents, gained more, so therefore a profit was made. The master is very pleased with what the servant with five talents accomplished and calls him a good and faithful servant. When something is good, it is suitable, agreeable and pleasant. It has a specific result. Faithful people are steadfast, loyal, disciplined and constant. Are there areas in your life where you need to show some discipline or steadfastness?

_____

_____

_____

_____

Verses 22-23, tells how the faithful servant with two talents received two more talents. The servant with one talent, offers his explanation in the next verses, 24 and 25 as to what happened with his talent. Who was he to assume anything about the master? He stated that he was afraid. Afraid is being filled with fear, concern, or regret. You can't use your fear of the unknown to keep you from doing what the Lord has said or keep you from moving to the next level in God. The master responds to this servant by calling him wicked and lazy. Laziness is the inability to act promptly or speedily when action is called for. Are you lazy? Are you moving slowly in accomplishing things that were prophesied over you or placed within your heart years ago?

God always wants a return on his investment in you. Just like when you invest your money, you want to make a profit on it. God is the same with you! When he gives you talents and gifts, He wants them to be used to build His kingdom. When you don't use what he has given you, you run the risk of losing what you have. The story ends in verse 28, where the servant that had the one talent, had it taken away from him and given to the faithful servant, who already had ten talents. The moral of the story is whomever maximizes what they have, can gain more talents to be used in God's kingdom.

Jesus is the man who went on the journey back to the Father. He has entrusted you with gifts and talents, according to your ability. He will want to know if you maximized your life while here on earth. Did you have and multiply what you had or did you hide your gifts and talents from the world? Your ultimate goal would be to have him say to you, "Well done good and faithful servant; enter into the promise that I have prepared for you."

Pause and take an internal assessment and be honest with yourself and ask: Am I really maximizing in areas of my life? Am I taking my five talents to make five more talents, or am I taking my one talent and just sitting, waiting, hiding, hoping, and wishing to do more, wishing to be more, wishing to have more. God is asking what are you waiting on or who are you waiting on? **It's Time to Move!** He has put too much knowledge and expertise inside you for you to keep it hidden. He has given you ideas, strategies, business plans and even books that can impact the world! It's time to maximize where you are in life, so that you can begin to walk in the overflow that he has planned for you. If you obey his Word, heed his instructions, and follow his plan, you can live a successful life and become your Best U!

Step 4: Make It Happen: Moving Towards Your Best U!
Learn How to Maximize! Maximize! Maximize!

What areas of your life need to be maximized?

_____

_____

_____

_____

_____

_____

_____

REAL DEAL TALK

My husband is an excellent teacher and preacher of the gospel. Early on as ministry partners, I learned that I had to be myself! I recognize that I maximize my gifts better in a workshop session on a Saturday morning or in a multi-purpose room at the Boys and Girls Club. My style of ministry and approach is different, but the effectiveness of each of our ministries reaches the intended audience. I don't try to compete with him! I want my style of ministry to complete God's plan for us as a couple in ministry.

Chapter 5
The Big C.H.O.P.

"He was despised and rejected by mankind, a man of suffering, and familiar with pain." Isaiah 53:3

Have you ever struggled in your life trying to please others, rather than trying to please yourself? Was there ever a point in your life where you wanted to just make others happy, rather than making yourself happy? I was at that point in my life. I wanted to make sure other's perceptions about me were more important than what I thought about myself. Perceptions are defined as thoughts, beliefs, or opinions that people have, based upon what **they** believe is acceptable. People often find themselves stuck in life, incapable of moving beyond the perceptions of others. If you get fed up on living this way, then a Big C.H.O.P. is needed. A Big C.H.O.P. means: **Choosing Happiness Over Perceptions.**

I personally can identify with trying to live up to the perceptions of other people, and it made me feel *inadequate, undervalued, scrutinized, insignificant,* and *defeated*. Finally, when I **C**hose to do in life what made me **H**appy **O**ver what other people's **P**erceptions were, I felt great! It was as if I was finally free to be me! However, my C.H.O.P. led to isolation, competition, and even jealousy by those closest to me.

Making a choice to be different also brought about some level of controversy. Individuals connected to me have even told me to my face that they don't like me. Even though this is unfortunate, I have to continue moving forward and doing what God desires for my life, my marriage, my family, and my career. Whenever you choose to be more in life, to do more, to have more, and to go further than those around you, expect it to be unsettling to them. You are a constant reminder of what they wish they could do or wish they can have. People sometimes have a hard time dealing with the fact you are happy with the life choices you have made. Yes, it might not work for them, but it works for you. It's your life, not theirs!

Comparatively, one of the most controversial figures in the New Testament was Jesus Christ. He did what he wanted to and was not afraid of other people's perceptions of him. Yes, he was loved by many, but he was also hated by those from within the religious community. Many of the religious leaders (i.e.: Scribes, Pharisees and Chief Priests) hated Jesus because he was an example of what they could have been, had they been willing to step outside the box of their old traditional mindsets. They opposed his teaching, his rationale and his ministry style. They tried to shut him up and shut him down! They wanted to get rid of him, but Jesus Christ lived to please God and to execute God's plan to redeem mankind back to God. When he made the decision to do what made God happy, that's when the hatred and isolation came.

One major point in reaching personal happiness comes through having spiritual happiness, which can be found in an intimate relationship with God. God provides a formula of happiness through his word, where he gives the standard of his expectations for his children. The following are four things that God desires for you to have and do while on earth:

<u>LIVE, INCREASE, ENTER AND POSSESS</u>

To live, increase, enter and possess has always been his original plan for mankind. In Genesis Chapter 1, we see the process in which God went through to create everything, including man. He made mankind in his image and likeness.

LIVE

And the LORD God formed man of the dust of the ground, and breathed into his nostrils the breath of life; and man became a living soul. Genesis 2:7 (KJV)

The traditional definition of the word live is to be alive or to have life. Live can also mean to have a life rich in experience. Do you desire a life that is rich in experience? The only way to have experience in something is to either go through it or to observe others.

EXPERIENCE CAN BE ACHIEVED IN TWO WAYS

1. Watching and observing others can be a real life experience: When you observe how someone dealt with their situation, you can quickly learn what worked or did not work

2. Having first-hand experience: Sometimes you can observe what other people went through and you still don't learn the lesson, and then it becomes first-hand knowledge for you, once you experience it.

Having a rich life means having abundant possessions, especially material wealth. God not only wants you to have a life that is rich, but also full and satisfying - not just rich in material things, but to be rich in him. To walk in your purpose for which he had created you and to fulfill your life destiny is the ultimate goal. That is the life that he wants you to have! I personally have begun living a rich life since I have been walking in my purpose. I am passionate about seeing others, especially young adults, become their best in all they do. I currently serve as a community mentor for four organizations, where I provide empowerment sessions. The students learn about becoming their best: Spiritually, Physically, Emotionally, Mentally and Professionally.

INCREASE

And God blessed them, and God said unto them, Be fruitful, and multiply, and replenish the earth, and subdue it: and have dominion over the fish of the sea, and over the fowl of the air, and over every living thing that moveth upon the earth. Genesis 1: 28 (KJV)

Increase means to become progressively greater in size, amount, or intensity. Little by little, you should make and see progress. Your life today should not be the same as it was five, ten, or even twenty years ago. Enlarging yourself by growing in your knowledge of God is a great way to increase the quality of your life. As I have invested in my relationship with God, I have experienced greater impact with my ministry. When I first began in ministry, my level of confidence was low. The more my confidence in God increased, the more progressive I became in my inspirational and empowerment sessions. As a result, I am more engaged with my audience. When I go back and compare participant comments from my earlier workshops with the comments that I currently receive, a majority of them felt very engaged in the session and very empowered in the subject matter.

ENTER

And the LORD God planted a garden eastward in Eden; and there he put the man whom he had formed. Genesis 2:8 (KJV)

Entering involves going or coming into something or fulfilling a part. You have a responsibility to reach your life purpose and obtaining the meaning for your existence. To enter requires movement or action. Did you notice the subliminal message, **Move U!**

on the front cover of the book? In order for you to obtain your life goals, you must move forward! When you begin to move towards your best, you will be able to obtain all that you were destined to have! Your life will continue to get better as you apply movement in all areas of your life. Movement should be measurable which means you should see substantial growth in your spiritual life, personal life, emotional stance, career development and physical well-being!

When I shifted my thinking towards better health, I begin to enter into a new dimension of functioning. I realized that it was possible for me to reach my weight loss goals and to move myself towards becoming my best me!

POSSESS

And God blessed them, and God said unto them, Be fruitful, and multiply, and replenish the earth, and subdue it: and have dominion over the fish of the sea, and over the fowl of the air, and over every living thing that moveth upon the earth. Genesis 1:28 (KJV)

When you possess something, it means you have control over it, it does not have control over you! God wants you to take control over those aspects in your mind, heart and body that have been spiraling out of control for many years. So, how do you take control of your life? By applying God's word to receive practical solutions to your situation.

When I decided to acknowledge some areas of my life that were spiraling out of control, that's when true change occurred. When I decided to address them honestly, it allowed me to be in control of my life, rather than life controlling me. Learning how to control my own thoughts and feelings has moved me towards being successful in my life endeavors.

As you take control of your life, it's now more important than ever to utilize that control wisely. Maximize your control by utilizing your time wisely. Time is not promised to anyone. Keeping your true purpose as your catalyst for living is very important. I personally don't want to leave this earth not having fulfilled my God given assignment to the best of my ability. I also don't want to ever have any regrets about what I could have accomplished. This too should be your goal - to do what you were **Born to Do, and Do it Every day** until your assignment on this earth has been completed! Don't die with your purpose not being fulfilled. Don't die with your gifts and talents not being used in the earth realm. Each day that you live is an excellent opportunity to give back to the universe. Many individuals have gone to their graves with so many talents and gifts they never tapped into. Don't miss this season of your life!

When you begin to talk about seasons, you must look at the four natural ways in which seasons occur: SPRING, SUMMER, FALL and WINTER. Each of these four seasons occur every three months and have specific characteristics and features that are only relevant for that time. That is what a season is - a time characterized by a particular circumstance or feature. So when you think of spring, what comes to mind? I think of hearing the birds singing, a freshness in the air and the flowers beginning to bud. Spring is a time of growth and development. Are you growing and developing in the things of God? Are you embracing a new way of thinking? Sometimes your biggest holdup in life is U! It is not about your own way of seeing things; it's about God's way and Godly order. There was a time that I could not move into the next phase in my life because of the fear of failure. I thought that doing something new would take me out of my comfort zone. Once I actually did it, I discovered it was not as bad as I thought it would be.

The second season of the year is summer. This is the period between spring and fall where it is the hottest part of the year. During the summer, a lot of people take time to relax, go on vacation, and rest from their labors of the spring. This is a time of increasing maturity, especially for students in school. A lot of times, kids return to school after the summer, a little taller, a litter bigger, a little different than when they left in the spring. Maturity shows signs of growth. As a Christian, are you showing signs of growth? You should be growing and developing in the things of God. If you are growing in the things of God, you should see change.

After summer, comes autumn or fall. This is a time when the leaves on the trees begin to change their color. It also becomes cooler outside and the heat from the hustle and bustle of life begins to decrease. As things start to slow down, it is a time of reflection and possible change as the individual may begin to see themselves in a different light. Is God challenging you to change some aspects of your life?

The final season of the year is winter. As you know, winter is the coldest part of the year, which has periods of inactivity. This is the time in which animals hibernate, people want to stay indoors, the tree leaves fall off and die and there is decay all around. Decay occurs when there is a decline in strength, soundness, prosperity and excellence. Even when there are times in your life where movement seems impossible, you must ***KEEP ON MOVING FORWARD.*** Don't die in your winter season in life. Begin to look forward to spring where you will have life again. Look forward to experiencing the happiness of growing and developing in the things of God. Choosing to be happy and living to please God will allow you to **Move Towards your Best U!**

Step 5: Make It Happen: Moving Towards Your Best U!

Do you need to **C**hoose **H**appiness **O**ver **P**erceptions?

You have allowed the following perceptions to keep you from moving forward with your life:

_____

_____

_____

_____

_____

_____

_____

<u>REAL DEAL TALK</u>

If you have ever been rejected, it's one of the hardest experiences to have. **REJECTION HURTS**, *especially if it comes from people within your inner circle of family and/or friends. I know what it personally feels like to not be accepted, treated unfairly, and to not be a favorite. For many years of my life, I accepted my membership in the* **NOT ENOUGH CLUB**. *As a member of the Not Enough Club, I was the following:*

Not Good Enough

Not Thin Enough

Not Pretty Enough

Not Light-Skinned Enough

Not Smart Enough

Not Rich Enough

Not Liked Enough

Not Favored Enough

One day, I decided to cancel my membership in this club. I decided to join another club – **THE I AM ENOUGH CLUB**! *This club had different members who accepted me for who I was, and I absolutely am glad that I moved on with my life. In this club, I have individuals who have been strategically placed in my life to help build me up. They value who I am and what I have to offer! Of course, controversy came as a result of me changing clubs. People didn't and still don't like it, but I am perfectly fine with it. Their part in my life story has helped shape me into the woman that I have become today!*

Chapter 6
Becoming a Person on the Move

"Do you not know that your bodies are temples of the Holy Spirit, who is in you, whom you have received from God? You are not your own; you were bought at a price. Therefore honor God with your bodies." 1 Corinthians 6:19-20

> **Disclaimer: This chapter is not intended as a substitute for the medical advice of physicians. The reader should regularly consult a physician in matters relating to his/her health and particularly with respect to any symptoms that may require diagnosis or medical attention.**

It was a clear and sunny day, and my family and I were on our summer vacation. Each year we try to take our children to a destination spot, alternating one year as an educational trip with the following year as a fun trip. Generally, on the educational trips, we visit historical places to include museums and science related locations. Our fun trips usually involve a theme park or a trip to the beach. On this particular fun vacation, we chose a full day at a theme park. Of course, theme parks have all sorts of rides and adventures for the entire family.

While growing up, I was adventurous, so whenever I visited a theme park, I would ride the daring rides, including roller coasters. I remember riding a few roller coasters over and over again. Sometimes eight to ten times in a row. Standing in a long line in the hot July heat was well worth the thrill that the ride provided me. I honestly enjoyed that funny feeling that I would get in my stomach as the roller coaster would make sharp turns and drop quickly from a higher altitude. I had no fear on these rides and looked forward to the opportunity to ride. The higher the thrill level, the more I wanted to ride it. I especially wanted to ride the ones that took me upside down, where I could see my feet go over my head as we looped around and around. On this particular vacation, my husband suggested that we ride one of low level thrill attractions.

This is about the extent of his thrill ride adventures. He doesn't generally ride roller coasters; oh, let me re-phrase that; he will ride the kiddie coasters with our children on occasion. So he and I stood in line for a few minutes, and, at the appropriate time, proceeded to our seats to begin the ride. He instantly gets into his seat, buckles up, and waits for the ride to begin. I go to my seat, sit down, grab the seat belt, and guess what, I can't get it to clasp. I pull and pull, but I can't get it to budge. It didn't clasp because I was **TOO FAT FOR THE RIDE!** The ride operator came over and also tried to buckle it and was unable to do it as well. So he politely said, "Sorry ma'am you will need to exit the ride. Oh man; boy was I so embarrassed. I remember walking towards the exit, and I went and sat down.

I watched as my husband went around and around on the ride, having fun, while I sat with tears rolling down my cheeks. I never shared with him exactly what happened, but I knew in that moment a change had to occur, and I was determined the next time that we went to an amusement park, I would be able to ride any ride that I wanted to! When I reached this point in my life, in order for me to be all that God had called for me to be, I had to mentally shift my thinking about my health and my attitudes towards fitness. When I reached the point of **ENOUGH IS ENOUGH**, I was able to make long term changes to my overall well-being.

I can recall additional situations where I experienced, I was

TOO FAT TO FIT! I call these my ***SEATBELT EXTENDER EXPERIENCES.*** If you have ever flown on an airplane, you are familiar with a seatbelt extender. When the flight attendant does their flight demonstration about the safety and emergency procedures of the aircraft, they use a sample seat belt to demonstrate how to buckle and unbuckle the seatbelt. Seatbelts are required for every passenger aboard a flight. For larger passengers, this seatbelt extender can also be used to connect the existing seat belt to the extender so they can be buckled in. I would like to share with you my three Seatbelt Extender Experiences:

SITUATION #1

I was traveling with a group of my co-workers on an hour and fifteen-minute flight to a conference. My seat on the plane was assigned next to one of my colleagues. I couldn't get my seat belt to fasten, and, because I was embarrassed to ask for the extender, I rode the whole flight with my jacket in my lap to conceal the fact that my seat belt was unfastened. I was willing to jeopardize my safety worrying about what my colleague would think of me asking for the extender.

SITUATION #2

Again, traveling along for work, I proceeded to go to my assigned seat. Since I knew I would need the extender, I pressed the little button above my seat to get the flight attendant's attention. She looked my way, and I thought she was coming to see what I needed; instead, she said out loud, "I'll bring you one of those things." She must have seen me struggling to try to get the seat belt fastened. I am unsure. All I know is that I felt all eyes were on me, and I was so embarrassed.

SITUATION #3

After my experience with situation #2, I decided, going forward, I would ask the flight attendant as soon as I entered the plane for the seatbelt extender. Since I am a frequent flyer, on most airlines, I receive priority boarding. Priority boarding allows me to be one of the first groups to enter the plane. On this flight, I was one of the first 20 passengers to board, so as I entered the plane, I asked the flight attendant for the seat belt extender. He agreed to give me one. Well, I waited and waited and waited for him to bring it. He kept assisting everyone else with their overhead luggage and walking back and forth, up and down the aisles. When everyone had boarded, he flamboyantly walked towards me and said "Here you go," in a very loud voice. Once again, I felt all eyes were on me. I told him, "I don't need it!" I was going to make sure that my seat belt was going to fasten, so I sucked in with all of my might long enough to hear the seatbelt click, and then determined that a change in my life needed to occur, so a seatbelt extender would not be needed in the first place. I needed to become a person on the move! I needed to lose weight, and that would solve the problem!

When I was a size 30/32, yes I actually wore a size 30 in women's pants, I would always scan the room that I entered to see if I was the largest person in the room. Over 75% of the time, I was. When I saw someone larger than me, it made me feel better about my fatness. Really, there was nothing great about being morbidly obese. When I discovered that I was the largest person, at times I felt ashamed and embarrassed. Even if you have never struggled with your weight, you can still identify with the feeling of what it feels like to have your life out of control in areas, such as gambling, drug or alcohol dependency, excessive shopping, fornication, hoarding, smoking, pornography, adultery, sexting, poor money management, lying, and gossiping to name a few. What do you struggle with?

_____

_____

_____

For many of you, you already know you have been at this stage in life long enough, and it's time to move! You have been at this same level physically, spiritually, mentally, emotionally and professionally, for some time now and it's time to go to another level. It's time to experience another dimension of living. How many of you can identify with the experience of a tugging? Could it be that God is trying to get your attention to say, **"GET UP AND MOVE TOWARDS YOUR BEST U?"** Now is the time to move on with your life. Staying in a fixed mindset, not growing or maturing, can stunt one's growth. Are there areas within your life that desperately need some movement? Is it in your relationships, spirituality, career or within your physical body?

I recall several years ago when our nation experienced the horrific aftermath of Hurricane Katrina in the city of New Orleans. I remember seeing on the news the tremendous loss of lives and property. After the hurricane passed through the city, some inhabitants still remained in the area. The mayor, at the time, got on national television and addressed those residents who refused to evacuate. He expressed how he understood the area held many memories; yes, this is where their homes once stood, but it was time to leave so they could begin to rebuild the city. Sounded pretty reasonable; just move out to begin life again. Surprisingly, over

10,000 residents refused to leave as instructed. As a result of their unwillingness to evacuate, they exposed themselves to an environment that was full of waste, surrounded by dead bodies, stinking sewage, stagnant/stale water and a hot and muggy climate. Why do you sometimes choose to remain in situations that you know are detrimental to your health, body, mind, or spirit and are not good for you?

_____

_____

_____

_____

Some reasons people may chose to remain may include: fear, confusion, the opinions of others or stubbornness. For me, I chose not take care of myself because I did not truly tap into my self-value or self-worth. It was easy to hide behind the fat rather than face myself in the mirror, as to who I truly was, and, most importantly, that I was God's original creation!

My hope for you as you are reading this book is that you will embrace God's original purpose for your life and that you do not subject yourself to the insanity of re-living the Katrina experience in your own life. Oh, you can easily say, "That would never happen to me" however, some of you are living your own Katrina experience that is:

FULL OF WASTE Waste is that which is not good for use; that's why the body has to get rid of it; it serves no purpose. Are you involved in situations that are not good for you and full of garbage and sewage?

SURROUNDED BY DEAD THINGS

I can imagine the residents seeing dead bodies and dead animals floating in the water around them. Are you in a dead relationship? A dead relationship is deprived of life and lacks the power to move.

STINKS

When something stinks, it has a strong and offensive odor. Does your attitude or behavior sometimes stink?

STAGNANT/STALE

Water that is not flowing becomes stale. One can become stagnant or stale in many areas of functioning. Are you stale physically, spiritually, emotionally, mentally or professionally?

HOT AND UNCOMFORTABLE

When something is hot, it contains an uncomfortable degree of heat. What are you experiencing that has become too hot for to handle?

Do you want to do what it takes to move on with your life? God wants you to take control of your life; get yourself together and **LIVE**! God has given insight in his word on how to better your life. **He wants you to Move Towards your Best U!** The key is to have the desire to advance and to become better. Don't become distracted about what others may think. People can make you see yourself so much differently than how God sees you. That is why you can't worry about folks, their comments or opinions. You go on, and do what God is instructing you to do. As you are manifesting, they will sit in amazement. If your plans are larger than anything they have ever done, then prepare for opposition. You must have the confidence that in spite of what others may say, you are more than a conqueror.

Once you have decided to move, don't be afraid. Remember God has your back. Choosing not to move when prompted can cause you to miss out on what God has in store for you. When God says move and you continue to remain in your stuff, you can end up not walking in your full potential! **Do you want to change your current state of functioning?** Dare to do something different within your life. Insanity is doing the same thing but desiring a different result. **Make it Happen and Move Towards your Best U!**

I took my own advice and decided to become a person who is physically on the move. I incorporated tips which have enabled me to live my best life yet!I have lost over *80 pounds* thus far, and I am doing my own K.I.S.S. Plan!

This is how I looked when my life was out of control at a size 30/32!

This is how I looked when I took control of my life!!
Photo taken April 2016

I am still moving towards reaching my overall weight loss goal! I am excited to share with you these six tips that have helped me become a person on the move:

TIP #1:	MAKE IT A LIFESTYLE CHANGE NOT "I'M ON A DIET"
TIP #2	TAKE ONE DAY AT A TIME
TIP #3	KEEP A PAIR OF SNEAKERS IN THE CAR
TIP #4	KEEP A FOOD JOURNAL
TIP #5	DEVELOP A SUPPORT NETWORK
TIP #6	HAVE A SNACK PLAN

TIP # 1: MAKE IT A LIFESTYLE CHANGE NOT "I'M ON A DIET"

When being healthy becomes a lifestyle, you learn how to eat things that you love, but you are able to do so in moderation. A diet generally restricts some food groups, and the individual ends up feeling deprived, and then, when the opportunity comes, they may not utilize self-control and end up over indulging. That was me several years ago. I tried every major diet out there. I would get temporary results but would find myself in the cycle of my weight going up and down. When I made the decision to live a healthy lifestyle each day, I was able to obtain the results I was seeking all those years.

The following is an example of a lifestyle change: *I recently attended my company's Annual Leadership Conference. This conference is where our entire Region of 180+ members come together to celebrate wins from the previous fiscal year. This event is a time of food, fun and socialization. The food is generally the highlight of the conference. We have unlimited access to very tasty breakfast, lunch and dinner menus. In years past, I indulged myself so much with the food that I would be miserable. And the majority of the time, we are sitting in seminars and sessions with no physical activity throughout the entire day. By the time I returned to my hotel room, late in the night, I would be exhausted and go straight to bed. This year I did something a little different:*

> *-I decided only to eat salads and vegetables for lunch and dinner. No pasta or bread for me. I even skipped the dessert bar.*
>
> *-I only drank water and unsweetened tea. I had unlimited access to soft drinks, juices and even alcoholic beverages, but water was my best friend!*

- *I planned to go to the hotel gym during the cocktail hour, but the hotel gym was empty, and I didn't feel safe being in there alone. So as my coworkers were socializing and drinking, I returned to my hotel room, found an exercise video on YouTube and worked out the entire cocktail hour.*

- *Whenever we had a break and even after eating lunch, I spent my time walking thru the lobby, event halls and even outside the hotel. I kept my feet moving.*

- *I packed my healthy snacks from home and brought them to the conference, so I could avoid snacks that were not healthy for me.*

- *A breakfast bar of eggs, sausage and bacon and other items were provided. Now, I have to admit, the aroma was very inviting. Over in the corner, they had a cereal table. With a smile on my face, I found a box of my favorite Kashi Cereal, grabbed a bowl, spoon and milk and returned to my hotel room to enjoy my breakfast. Out of sight, out of mind, worked for me.*

- *As I was walking through the hotel, several peers asked, "What are you doing?" They saw me in my business casual clothes with sneakers on my feet. I said to them, "I'm going for a walk!" I had one co-worker say to me, "Girl, that's crazy!" I told her, "it might look crazy to you, but I must get my steps in!"*

- *Upon returning home, I was anxious to jump on my scale. Normally, in years past, I regretted returning home to see how much I gained. Depending on the length of the conference, it could be anywhere from 2 to 5 pounds. For the first time ever, when I stepped on the scale, I LOST WEIGHT at this Leadership Conference!! It just proves that when healthiness becomes a lifestyle, you stick to your plans, and you can get the results that you seek.*

TIP #2 TAKE ONE DAY AT A TIME

Remember that you did not get this way overnight. It was a result of many years of not taking care of yourself. If you have a goal of losing a whole lot of weight, it becomes easier to break it down into smaller goals rather than focusing on the larger number. If one hundred pounds is the goal, striving to reach twenty-five pounds at a time is a more realistic approach to losing that amount of weight. Take it one day at a time, and make the healthiest choices each day.

TIP #3 KEEP A PAIR OF SNEAKERS IN THE CAR

I don't leave my house without either wearing a pair of sneakers or having a pair in my trunk. Every opportunity I get to walk, I seize it. Parking further in the parking lot at my destination gives me an opportunity to get more steps in. It is recommended that an individual walk 10,000 steps a day for maximum heart health. You may think that is a whole lot of steps, but, if you break it down to smaller walking segments, you will quickly see 10,000 steps as very easy to obtain. Purchasing a pedometer will help keep you on track in the counting of the steps. There are many versions available, and also there are ones that connect to your smart phone, such as Fit Bit. The most steps that I have ever taken were 30,000 steps in one day. I broke it down into three 10,000 step sessions. Walking is a cheap and safe way to get in the number of steps recommended in a day.

TIP #4 KEEP A FOOD JOURNAL

Keeping a record of everything that you eat will help keep you accountable. There are many ways to track your food intake, from writing it down in a journal to using an app on your computer or smart phone. When I first began my food journal, I used a pocket sized calendar to record all of my food intake for the day. It included the item and the caloric intake. I now record my food electronically on an app called My Fitness Pal. Keeping a detailed record allows me to see what I am eating and if it is helping me lose weight. The journal is only effective as long as you record everything. If what you eat has a calorie, then it must be included. No EXCEPTIONS!

TIP #5 DEVELOP A SUPPORT NETWORK
There are always other people who are in the same boat as you. Your support network can be friends, family, co-workers or neighbors. Being accountable to them and providing encouragement to each other, helps on those days you may feel unmotivated to continue your healthy journey. I am a member of a Walking Club called The Faith Steppers. We have daily and weekly challenges that we complete, and we also, at times, compete with each other to see who can take the most steps in a day, during the work week or over the weekend. It is a friendly way to stay engaged on our journeys and to have someone literally cheering you on as you complete the walking challenges.

TIP #6 HAVE A SNACK PLAN
Around 3:00 pm each workday, I use to visit the vending machine in my company's breakroom. My favorite item of choice was a Snicker's Bar. It was something about how the chocolate, caramel and peanuts tasted. I absolutely loved the crunch of the nuts and the smoothness of the chocolate. If I continued to eat a snickers bar each day, it would not help me reach my weight loss goals. In order for me to have healthier snacks available, I organize and bring my snacks from home. My snacks include items such as: Fruit, string

cheese, nuts, granola bars and popcorn. Preparing them at home saves money and keeps me from visiting the vending machine!

Making the decision to become a person on the move has affected all areas of my life in a positive manner. I sleep better, have more energy, my clothes fit better, and my stress levels have decreased. I am so thankful that I took my initial steps to move towards wellness. Remember you only have one chance to live this life, and taking care of your body is an excellent way to show reverence and worship unto God!

Step 6: *Make It Happen: Moving Towards Your Best U!*
Are you moving or are you stagnant?

_____

_____

_____

_____

_____

_____

Moving yields tremendous results.

What areas of your life need movement?

_____

_____

_____

_____

_____

What are your short term goals?

_____

_____

_____

_____

_____

What are your long term goals?

_____

_____

_____

_____

_____

REAL DEAL TALK

There are times I don't want to go to the gym and I think about young people that I knew who died prematurely, as a result of unhealthy lifestyles. I also think about my children and the example that I want to set for them in reference to having a healthy lifestyle. I must do this, not just for me, but for the generations that will come after me!

There are times in which I look at the elliptical machine and say "I'm really not feeling you today!" One thing I have come to realize is results are very motivational. The more results I achieve motivates me to keep pushing forward. I am reminded at the end of the day, I am achieving my desired results.

One time I saw a guy, at the gym, who was really serious about his workout. I said to him "Wow, one day I hope to be able to work out like you are doing." He said, "That can happen; just keep showing up every day and it will." I have never forgotten those words and what have I been doing? I have been showing up, been committed to my exercise routine, and I am so much closer in reaching my goal!

Chapter 7
This is how you DO IT in the Workplace!

"...do it all for the glory of God." I Corinthians 10: 31b

We have spent time up to this point focusing on becoming your best in your spiritual, emotional and physical being. Now, let's **Move Towards your Best U!** in your professional career. Whether you are starting your career or have been working in your profession for some time, being your Best U! in the workplace can be a very fulfilling experience.

I've had the opportunity to work in various trades that include: retail, fast food, grocery, non-profit and state government. Each of these experiences were unique, and I learned so much about myself during the process. I can honestly say my current career status highlights my talents and gifts. I have followed an intentional path, which has enabled me to become successful in my role as a Store Manager and Regional Human Resources Facilitator. I am passionate about training and developing people, and this passion resonates in all aspects of my current leadership position. I enjoy helping others achieve their career objectives. The following are six tips I have incorporated in my leadership roles over the years and I know these tips can help you become your Best U! in the workplace.

TIP #1:	INVITE GOD TO BE A PART OF YOUR WORKDAY
TIP #2:	ASPIRE TO YOUR NEXT POSITION
TIP #3:	LEAVE YOUR PERSONAL LIFE AT HOME
TIP #4:	HAVE A MENTOR/BECOME A MENTOR
TIP #5:	BE A PROBLEM SOLVER, NOT A PROBLEM SPOTTER
TIP #6:	REMEMBER YOUR ULTIMATE BOSS IS GOD

TIP #1: INVITE GOD TO BE A PART OF YOUR WORKDAY

It is very important to invite God to be a part of your workday. I know with an extreme level of assurance that I have to rely on God's wisdom and direction to help lead and guide me each day while I am at work. During your personal devotional time, PRIOR to going to work, is an excellent opportunity to set your tone for the workday. It is very important to be in the right mindset before arriving to the job. On the job, as you know, you are faced with so many different people whose values, lifestyles, or ethics may or may not be similar to yours. Being prayerful is key in helping you overcome the obstacles you will face throughout the day.

There have been many times over the years when I needed help with something that I was working on. While sitting at my desk, I have asked God to help me with my projects. I have asked him to give me ideas to enhance my creativity and to give me the necessary exposure that I needed. Earlier in my career, I was given a task to come up with a creative idea to market a company initiative. God had given me an idea to hang an attention getting display at the entrance of the establishment. My co-workers laughed at the display and said they thought it was a silly idea. I knew the idea was inspired by God, and I kept the display on view. A few weeks later, our Regional Vice President (RVP), came to the store for a visit. For those of you familiar with retail, a visit from the RVP or higher ranking individuals within the company is an important visit. She walked by my display and expressed to me how much she really liked it. She shared how my creativity would intrigue the customer's interest in the product, and she celebrated what I had done! As a result of my God inspired idea, our store achieved its benchmark for the initiative.

TIP #2: ASPIRE TO YOUR NEXT POSITION

If you have aspirations to advance your career, then tip #2 is just for you. It is important to already think proactively (anticipate problems and show initiative), act professionally and communicate effectively like the boss before the opportunity for advancement arises. I was very upfront in my interview with my current employer that I had aspirations to become more than an Assistant Manager (ASM) with the company. I was hired as an ASM over Human Resources (HR) and Operations. At the time, I had over thirteen years of experience in the Human Resources field. A successful career in Human Resources demands pro-active thinking, acting professionally, and a high level of interpersonal communication and interaction skills.

Most promotions in our company occur when an individual is recognized by their current supervisor for having the capacity to:

a. Think and plan pro-actively

b. Demonstrate excellence

c. Inspire others to act accordingly

I was promoted from an ASM to a Store Manager (SM) because I demonstrated to my District Manager (DM) that I had the capacity to:

a. Help my store achieve the company's goals through thinking and planning pro-actively

b. Demonstrated a level of excellence which could be modeled by others

c. Inspired my team to follow my example through positive communication and reinforcement

My SM did not have to worry about any of the operations of the store when I was on duty. I took care of everything. I showed her that I was capable of functioning like a SM, while being in the ASM position. Functioning like a SM did not mean that I walked around with my chest out thinking I was somebody. No, quite the opposite! Functioning like a SM meant I was fully aware of all aspects of the business and I knew how to engage myself into every area of the business without making my boss feel like I was taking her job. I was pro-active in my thinking because I had a total store approach verses just thinking about my human resources area.

Functioning like a SM meant I was willing to inspire others to get the work load done, and I was willing to plan strategically and use sound judgment in my decision making processes. It also meant I needed to anticipate problems and set appropriate priorities for the day. Building a rapport, valuing diversity and having the ability to relate to people was key to me aspiring to the role of a SM before officially being promoted to the position. Having aspirations prepared me for the promotional opportunity, and I was able to have a smooth transition when I began working as a SM.

TIP# 3: LEAVE YOUR PERSONAL LIFE AT HOME

I always tell my staff that it is imperative when they enter into the building that anything they did or the problems they faced prior to arriving to work, should stay outside the job. Co-workers should not know every time you and your spouse have an argument or every time your child is disobedient. Outside problems should not affect your ability to work. When co-workers walk around broadcasting their problems, it can become a distraction to others and hinder productivity. If everyone is talking about your problems, who is actually working?

Here's an example that I heard once about what customers think when they shop at a retail establishment. When a consumer purchases a ticket to Walt Disney World, upon arriving at the theme park, their expectation is to experience the Walt Disney World brand. Disney's brand is a magical world where a "Kid can be a Kid". Therefore any employee who works for the theme park, must represent that brand regardless of their personal life outside of work. So the employee wearing the Mickey or Minnie Mouse costume must deliver the Walt Disney experience "where dreams come true." The children can care less about how the person wearing the costume is feeling; all they want is to get the everlasting memory of the experience.

In comparison, when your clients or customers come to your place of business, they can care less about what is going on in your personal life. At that moment, your role is to provide the best shopping experience possible! So smile (fake it if you have to), and give them what they want! Give your supervisor and co-workers what they want as well - a positive team player who delivers positive results, and not someone who complains about their personal life. Once your shift is over and you exit those doors, then you can continue to deal with your personal stuff. ***Don't bring it in; leave it at the door!***

Now, if you are experiencing extreme difficulties outside the workplace and you need to talk to someone about it, the appropriate way to handle it would be to talk to your supervisor or a member of the human resources team, not to your co-worker, who most likely can't help you anyway. Many companies provide resources such as an Employee Assistance Program, which helps employees deal with life problems outside of work.

TIP #4: HAVE A MENTOR/BECOME A MENTOR

All of my mentors over my career have helped me to become who I am in the workplace. A role of a mentor is to help the mentee grow professionally. Mentors provide advice on career options, offer feedback on areas for improvement, and are willing to share their experiences as examples to help the mentees make good decisions.

I have been blessed to have three professional mentors that have helped shape my current leadership style. They were each different in their working styles, but I have greatly benefited from watching and observing them in the workplace. They each challenged me to become my best and gave me feedback when I did not make the best choices. These phenomenal women took the time to teach me how to become successful, and I am grateful that our paths crossed. The following is a list of what I learned from my mentors. A successful leader must learn how to be:

MY MENTORS	CHARACTERISTICS
Mentor #1	Straight-forward and Transparent
Mentor #2	Knowledgeable and Laid Back
Mentor #3	Charismatic and Inspiring

Straight-forward

Speak the truth with your co-workers, especially when the truth will help them become better in their jobs. It does not benefit anyone if you are not authentic with your message.

Transparent

To be transparent is being honest about what worked and didn't work so others can learn from those successes and failures. Transparency doesn't involve you telling everyone everything about your experiences. It means that you are willing to share appropriate things at appropriate times.

Knowledgeable

Years of experience should allow a person to be well versed in their profession. For me, having the opportunity to learn the ins and outs of the business is very important. You should seize every chance to learn the business from those who have experienced it before you.

Laid Back

There are times to be serious, and there are times to loosen up. Learning when to apply these two approaches is vital in connecting to your co-workers. When deadlines are eminent, then of course you can't have a laid back approach. When goals have been met and the team deserves a little fun on the job, show your casual side but still be professional!

Charismatic

My charismatic mentor made her job seem like it was a breeze. Individuals with charisma have a personal quality of influence over a large number of people. She would often say that training was her passion, and I believe it to be so! She had a way of captivating her audiences with her messages. By the end of her presentations, I always felt empowered and determined to continue on.

Inspiring

Meeting individuals with inspiring lives can push you towards your own personal greatness. Any mentor that has experienced adversity and is still able to inspire is very motivating. My mentor, even as she was facing a medical challenge, continued to encourage me. Her heart was about serving others in spite of what she was going through.

Be a Mentor

Not only should you have a mentor on the job, but you should also become a mentor. Once you have become established within your career, always look to see who you can mentor to become better in their position. I am seen as a Human Resources Expert amongst my colleagues, so they are constantly asking my opinion on how to handle certain situations within their work environment. I provide them with insight from a HR perspective.

Over the span of my career, I have had the opportunity to mentor hundreds of people. This has been accomplished in several ways including being a Regional Facilitator, Community Mentor, Store Manager and personal one-on-one mentoring. Here are two examples of mentor/mentee relationships I have been involved in:

Mentee #1: A female associate who had been in management previously and was a part of one of my leadership teams, solicited my assistance when she felt she was ready for a promotion. I eagerly agreed to do everything that I could possibly do to assist her. She wanted to spend time with me to see how I was able to become the expert in my arena. I spent many hours coaching her in improving her professional skills. I provided opportunities for her to excel within our store location and gave her visibility outside of our store. There were times that she embraced my advice, and other times she did not agree with me. The process taught us both something. In the end, it all paid off; she was promoted and is currently very successful in her new position.

Mentee #2: I had a part-time female associate that would occasionally ask me questions and get my opinion on problems that she was experiencing at her full-time job. I would always answer her truthfully and provide a response based on my many years in management. When an opportunity came for her to be promoted on her full-time job, I encouraged her to go for it. Based on what I knew about her, I felt she would be an excellent candidate. I gave her a few interviewing tips, wrote her a letter of recommendation and answered some questions she had. She was able to get the promotion, and I was very happy for her. I had no idea I was her mentor, until one day, she asked to speak with me as I was leaving work. She began to share with me that I was an example of what inspired her to pursue management. She said, "If Felicia could do this and be successful, so can I." She thanked me for being such a positive example of a Minority in Management. She ended with, "What are you going to do next to be a blessing unto me? How is God going to use you in the future to bless me?" I told her I had to go and quickly write down what she had shared with me. As I sat in my car, I offered up thanks unto God for once again confirming that I was exactly where he needed me to be!

TIP# 5: BE A PROBLEM SOLVER, NOT A PROBLEM SPOTTER

Every day while at work, you may come across something that can be considered as a problem on the job. One of my biggest pet peeves is listening to a complainer. When I ask them, "What is your solution for the problem?" They generally don't have anything else to say. Having a solution to a problem shows your supervisor you have the ability to take initiative and possibly have a "Big Picture" mentality. Big picture thinkers operate outside of their assigned areas and are seen as forward thinking individuals. Whenever I consider an associate for a promotion, I am drawn to candidates which take initiative and have offered viable suggestions in the past. A simple idea that saves on productivity and enhances our best method practices is always welcomed. Are you a forward thinker? Are you the next boss in training?

TIP# 6: REMEMBER YOUR ULTIMATE BOSS IS GOD

God is My Chief Executive Officer (CEO). When I accepted God's intimacy invitation, I accepted his will for my life and followed his lead. As the CEO, his role is to lead and oversee the short and long term goals of my life. I am very respectful of my supervisors and leaders within my organization. I do value their opinions and thoughts about my career. Ultimately, my life is in God's hands. The plans that he has for me were formed a long time ago. *Jeremiah 29:11, states: For I know the plans I have for you," declares the LORD, "plans to prosper you and not to harm you, plans to give you hope and a future."* I am on his payroll, and I should do all things, including my secular job, unto his glory.

Since I work for him, I have a responsibility to let my light shine in the workplace. Letting my light shine does not mean that I go around and talk about God all day. No; it means that how I show up in the workplace should represent God in how I carry myself. People are always watching everything that is done on the job. They may or may not comment, but they are observing. Do you show up to work on time? Do you take your allotted time for your lunch and or breaks? Do you use your work computers, copiers, fax machine or office phone for work purposes only? How do you respond to your co-workers? How do you respond to customer complaints? How do you react to adverse situations? Are you pleasant, or do you talk to co-workers or customers in an unprofessional manner? Even in the workplace, it is very important that you display a Christian demeanor, if you are classifying yourself as a follower of Christ. **1 Corinthians 10: 31b, states: "do it all for the glory of God."** You have a responsibility to be his official representative and to make him proud!

STEP 7: *Make It Happen: Moving Towards Your Best U!*
Which of the six tips do you need to implement the most and why?

_____

_____

_____

_____

_____

_____

_____

_____

_____

REAL DEAL TALK

Over the twenty-seven plus years that I have been working, I can honestly say that I have some co-workers that have literally gotten on my last nerves. From those that thought they knew it all to those who never "pulled their weight." It was very frustrating to be on a team when the team members did not want to do what was right. In my mind, I was thinking that they are getting paid just like me to do the job, so they should just do it! I felt like I was doing the majority of the work on many projects, but they were getting the credit as well by the supervisor. But I can say now, having those experiences have taught me about what it takes to get a job done and has shaped my leadership style that I currently use with my team.

As a Manager, there is one thing that I do in every location that I am assigned to: I have learned how valuable it is to have a connection with each of my associates. John Maxwell says, **"People don't care how much you know until they know how much you care."** *This is so true! Over the years, I learned so much about people's children, grandchildren, spouses, trips they have been on and even their pets. I take the time to ask them about how things are going. For my students, I even inquire about how school is going for them. Remember people work for individuals and not for companies. Be the Boss that your employees want to work for!*

Chapter 8
Delayed but not Denied

"For my thoughts are not your thoughts, neither are your ways my ways," declares the Lord." Isaiah 55:8

What do you do if you are moving towards your Best U! and your life comes to a stop sign? You were doing everything you were supposed to, and, without warning, your plans came to a single screeching halt. There have been specific times in my professional career where things did not happen the way in which I wanted them to. I was delayed in manifesting my desired result. Was I happy about having to wait? Absolutely not, but the process of waiting made me a stronger individual, and, as a result, I was a more valuable contributor to my employer. Let's examine three of my human resources experiences where I was delayed in achieving my desired results.

Experience #1

I was working as a HR Assistant for a State Agency but desired to be promoted to a HR Manager or HR Director. I had been in the position for over two years and wanted to grow and expand into a more responsible role. For many months, I applied for HR positions within State Government. I went on several interviews, but no one would extend me an offer. I met all of the training and experience requirements but was not the most qualified for the job. After job searching for over a year, I was able to secure a HR Manager position outside of state government where I received a 50% increase in my salary. I would not have gotten anything close to that kind of salary by continuing to work in state government. I was temporarily delayed but not denied the HR position.

Experience #2

I was working in a HR Manager position but desired to be promoted to a District or Regional HR Position. After two and a half years in this role, I knew that I had it within me to be more influential on a higher level. I once again started to explore positions outside of the company. Nothing came open for me. About three years into the position, my company went through a major restructuring where over 1,800 HR Managers were laid off. This lay off included me. I was given an opportunity to apply for the vacant District and Regional HR positions. I interviewed for them both but did not get either. I ended up accepting the severance package and immediately began to look for another job. Two weeks before the severance package ended, I was offered the position as an ASM/HR Manager with an expanding company. I was temporarily delayed but not denied a position.

Experience #3

About one year after I was working as an ASM with my current employer, I had the desire to be promoted to the Store Manager position. My Store Manager at the time was transferred to another location. Her leaving the store opened up the opportunity for a current ASM to be promoted. I felt I had the necessary qualifications for the role. The selection process occurred, but I was not offered the position. I was a little disappointed, but I used the experience as a chance to grow more in my role as an ASM. I didn't become bitter or resented the co-worker that was promoted instead of me. As I shared in the previous chapter, I supported her and helped her accomplish the goals in which she had established for her store.

Approximately a year and a half later, another SM vacancy occurred within the district, and this time I was ready. I received the promotion, and it has been well worth the wait. My current role gives me the flexibility to do all of my desired HR roles, all rolled up into one position. I currently serve as a Store Manager and Regional HR Facilitator. As a Regional HR Facilitator, I am given the opportunity to travel all over the United States conducting specialized training in Customer Service, Leadership Development and Retail Store Development for Store Management Teams. I got the best job possible in one opportunity with a company that I thoroughly enjoy working for!

Comparatively, there is a story in the Bible that deals with an individual who was delayed in receiving the desires of her heart. Delay implies a holding back from completion or arrival. How many of you have been delayed before? You find yourself not getting exactly what you wanted, when you wanted it. It is as if something is standing in your way of achieving what is in your heart.

When something is denied, it is prevented from happening. An example of being denied would be if you apply for a Credit Card and they deny your application. Denial from that company means they are refusing to grant unto you the gratification of our desires, approval of the credit card. When a person is denied, it hurts! Disappointment and frustration causes people to want to throw in the towel and to give up. Let's look at a story in the Old Testament which involves an individual who was delayed in receiving her heart's desire.

There was a certain man… whose name was Elkanah. He had two wives; one was called Hannah and the other Peninnah. Peninnah had children, but Hannah had none. 1 Samuel 1:1-2

During this time in history, it was permissible for a man to have multiple wives. Having children during this time, meant the woman was successful in producing an offspring and even more specifically a male child was desired. A male child could continue the lineage of the father. If a woman could give her husband a child, she was considered great in that time.

Year after year this man went up from his town to worship and sacrifice to the LORD Almighty at Shiloh, where Hophni and Phinehas, the two sons of Eli, were priests of the LORD. Whenever the day came for Elkanah to sacrifice, he would give portions of the meat to his wife Peninnah and to all her sons and daughters. But to Hannah he gave a double portion because he loved her, and the LORD had closed her womb. 1 Samuel 1: 3-5

Elkanah was a wealthy man who was able to travel wherever he desired. Money was not a concern of his. When he went to the priest to offer his sacrifice, he would give a portion to Peninnah, but he would give a double portion to Hannah. Elkanah loved her, he favored her, he desired her, but GOD had shut up her womb. It is very obvious that Hannah had an issue in being able to conceive a child since Peninnah, Elkanah's other wife, was able to produce offspring for Elkanah. Hannah could not give him a child. God had created an issue of restriction in Hannah's life by shutting up her womb.

May I suggest some of the things that you are experiencing in your life are a result of God closing them off in order for Him to be your focus? Does God want you to turn to him for direction and to seek his will for your life?

Because the LORD had closed Hannah's womb, her rival kept provoking her in order to irritate her. 1 Samuel 1:6

1 Samuel Chapter 1 does not say it, but I am sure there were some conversations between Peninnah and Hannah, where Peninnah was taunting Hannah, saying "I can give Elkanah many

children; how many have you given him?" There is nothing that can irritate a person more than seeing someone else doing, having, obtaining, getting, and enjoying something they feel as though they should have. I am sure it sent Hannah to her breaking point.

This went on year after year. Whenever Hannah went up to the house of the LORD, her rival provoked her till she wept and would not eat. 1 Samuel 1:7

So the provoking and irritating went on for a while. Some of you have been going through your irritation with life for quite some time. Just when you think you have gotten yourself together, you find yourself in a delayed state of functioning.

Her husband Elkanah would say to her, "Hannah, why are you weeping? Why don't you eat? Why are you downhearted? Don't I mean more to you than ten sons?" 1 Samuel 1:8

Just as Hannah cried and cried and cried, many of you may cry as you sit and wait for the next move in your life. You have something in your heart that you desire to have. Some people close to you may ask "what's wrong with you?" Shouldn't you be content with what you already have? Elkanah had provided Hannah with so much of his wealth that he could not understand that she still wanted to give him a child. The desire she had was far greater than seeing the love that she already had in her life. Elkanah could not understand what Hannah was going through, just as there are some around you that don't understand what you are going through and what you are desiring out of life.

And she was in bitterness of soul, and prayed unto the Lord, and wept sore. 1 Samuel 1:10 (KJV)

If you ever interacted with a bitter person or if you have been a bitter person, it is a bad place to be in. Bitter means to exhibit intense animosity, resentment, or to be accompanied by severe pain or suffering. One does not want to be around a person who is bitter. Their countenance is unpleasant; they are constantly complaining, and nothing makes them happy. Hannah was very bitter. She resented Peninnah. Her rival, Peninnah represented something she could not have. **I am so glad that I did not turn bitter when I did not receive the promotion in the past, when my colleague did**! Once bitterness sets in, frustrations will be on the rise, and your way of coping is by crying much and praying to God. Hannah had many nights of wet pillows from her tears where she asked herself, *"WHY NOT ME LORD?"* How many nights are your pillows wet with tears as you think about where others are in life and you ask God, **WHY NOT ME LORD?"**

And she made a vow, saying, "O LORD Almighty, if you will only look upon your servant's misery and remember me, and not forget your servant but give her a son, then I will give him to the LORD for all the days of his life, and no razor will ever be used on his head." 1 Samuel 1:11

How many of you have made a promise to God right in your bedroom? God, if you get me out of this one, I promise I will _____. (You fill in the blank). God, if you get me out of debt, this time, I promise I will not go down this road again. God, if you give me this job, I promise I will do what I am supposed to do. God, if you give me a house or a new car, I promise I will take care of it. God, if you give me a mate, I promise I will treat him/her right. It sounds very familiar; many of you have made these promises knowing that only God can give you the solution that you seek.

As she kept on praying to the LORD, Eli observed her mouth. 1 Samuel 1:12

Important to note…SHE KEPT PRAYING!!! She did not stop even when there was no physical sign that God had heard her prayer. She kept praying even when the heartache, disappointment, and stress was very heavy. She kept praying even when others looked at her. She kept praying because she realized that she was temporarily delayed but felt that God was not going to DENY HER REQUEST!!! When I was desiring the promotions, I prayed to God quite frequently. My desire was that I would be in his will, and that my life would be pleasing unto him.

Hannah was praying in her heart, and her lips were moving but her voice was not heard. Eli thought she was drunk and said to her, "How long will you keep on getting drunk? Get rid of your wine. 1 Samuel 1:13-14

Are you waiting for God for your breakthrough? People can't understand how you keep speaking of the goodness of God when it looks like your situation is not changing. They are amazed that you keep praying when you don't see a change yet.

"Not so, my lord," Hannah replied, "I am a woman who is deeply troubled. I have not been drinking wine or beer; I was pouring out my soul to the LORD. Do not take your servant for a wicked woman; I have been praying here out of my great anguish and grief." 1 Samuel 1: 15-16

Set people straight! This craziness they think you possess is really you trying to get a hold of what God has for you. You are not drunk with wine, but you are drunk in your love for God and what you believe that he is going to do for you!!! Hannah let the priest know that she is there because she has experienced much anguish and grief. Grief can kill you. I have been there. When a person very close to me died several years ago, I had a very hard time dealing with it. No one really understood the depth of our relationship, even others close to me. Grief is defined as deep distress. It was a dark place in my life. It caused anguish, stress and it was a tough place to be in. It was only by God's grace that I survived that difficult time in my life, and I am able to share with others my story about how God brought me through it.

Eli answered, "Go in peace, and may the God of Israel grant you what you have asked of him." 1 Samuel 1:17

The priest hooked up with Hannah's faith and was in agreement with her to receive the blessing that she desired. You need to hook up with people that help you go towards the things of God, not away from them. Just as Eli was in agreement with Hannah, I am thankful that my husband encouraged me as I was going through my dark moments. He did not give up on me but spoke words to help push me forward and not backwards.

She said, "May your servant find favor in your eyes." Then she went her way and ate something, and her face was no longer downcast. 1 Samuel 1:18

After you have surrounded yourself with positive people, have received an encouraging word, things can start to look a little better. The text states that Hannah went on her way, ate some food and her countenance changed. When you have a different response, it is God's opportunity to give you a different outcome. When you stop feeling sorry for yourself and let go of baggage that holds you down, real progress can be achieved. If you change your thinking, hold your head up high, put that smile on your face and say, "Nothing is going to happen today that me and God can't handle together," that's when you will experience your breakthrough.

Early the next morning they arose and worshiped before the LORD and then went back to their home at Ramah. Elkanah lay with Hannah his wife, and the LORD remembered her. 1 Samuel 1:19

Worship is an act of expressing reverence to God. True worship is not manufactured; it is pure, natural and comes from your heart. God responds to your worship. When Hannah worshiped, God responded to her by opening up her womb. God remembered her and gave her the thing her heart desired.

So in the course of time Hannah conceived and gave birth to a son. She named him Samuel, saying, "Because I asked the LORD for him. 1 Samuel 1:20

Just as Hannah received her heart's desire, although it was

delayed, God did not deny her. God wants you to know the key to you receiving the thing in your heart is tied up in your worship, your true reverence of him, and the acceptance of the purpose he has in your life.

God has a purpose for your life, and the sooner you walk in that purpose the closer you are to living out that purpose. If you don't know what you were created to do, then seek his face, worship him, and he will lead you to the life that he has for you. Yes, you may have been delayed in receiving, but God will not deny what he has promised unto you!!! Begin to move into your next phase in life.

Step 8: Make It Happen: Moving towards your Best U!
Your promise may be delayed, but it won't be denied.

What areas of your life have you experienced a delay?

_____

_____

_____

_____

What are your feelings concerning the delay?

_____

_____

_____

_____

Have you become irritated or bitter? If so, what do you need to do in order to move forward in your life?

_____

_____

_____

_____

REAL DEAL TALK

There were times in which I left some of my interviews, and I felt really good about the process. I had answered all the questions appropriately, and I had felt a genuine rapport with the interviewers. I honestly did not like receiving those rejection letters in the mail that stated they were unable to offer me the position, and they had chosen another candidate. At times, that was devastating news, and I felt like I wasn't good enough for the positions. I knew I had a lot to offer to the right organization. That disappointment hurt. Looking back now, I realize that it was all about God's plan and God's timing! Not mine!

Chapter 9
Moving Towards WHOLENESS

"And we know that all things work together for good to them that love God, to them who are the called according to his purpose."
Romans 8: 28 (KJV)

As I began to reflect over my life and considered all the good, bad, trials, tribulations, successes and failures I have experienced, I came to the conclusion that all of them have made me become who I am today. It is so easy for me to celebrate the good experiences: Being accepted and graduating from college, getting married, having children, starting a church, becoming a home owner, becoming an entrepreneur and having the ability to travel across the country for my job and leisurely. But what about those not so good times: Being taunted and teased in high school, having suicidal thoughts as a teen, experiencing rejection from loved ones, having a miscarriage between the birth of my oldest son and my daughter, receiving an abnormal pap smear, discovering a small mass during my self-breast examination and being laid off from my job; looking back, all of these experiences worked out for my good. Without all of those experiences, I would not have a story to share. I would not be able to tell you how to **Move Towards your Best U!** Throughout this book, you have followed my life journey that has been a combination of many different circumstances and situations. I pray that you have been given tips and strategies to move towards all that God has for you!

Aspects of your life journey may be similar or different than mine. ***John 16:33b*, states: *In this world you will have trouble.*** As a human being, you are guaranteed to experience some trials and tribulations in life. *James 1: 2-3 as states: Consider it pure joy, my brothers and sisters, whenever you face trials of many kinds, because you know that the testing of your faith produces perseverance. Let perseverance finish its work so that you may be mature and complete, not lacking anything.* Now let's talk about what the scripture means.

Have you have ever experienced a trial in your life? A trial is defined as a test of faith, patience or endurance through suffering or temptation. A test is something that measures the skill, knowledge, intelligence or capacity of an individual. Just like in school, the teacher gives a test to see whether or not you have understood the subject matter. The goal should always be to score the highest possible on that assignment. Trials are very similar to tests. Trials are designed to test your understanding as an individual.

James 1:2 states, you should consider it a great joy when you have experience various trials. I don't know about you, but, when I have gone through a trial, I don't consider it a joy. His call for joy in the face of trials may seem shocking or even insensitive, but what James wants you to have is the joy in the **results** of the trials; it's not about the trials themselves. Even difficult times can produce good qualities such as endurance. When you endure, you undergo a hardship without giving in. What have you endured, survived or tolerated?

_____

_____

_____

_____

Have you ever experienced TRIALS that questioned your faith in God, your faith in self, your faith in other people?

_____

_____

_____

_____

_____

_____

_____

_____

_____

_____

_____

The frequency of and the length of a trial varies from individual to individual. But what do you do when your trial continues to linger on and on? It seems as soon as you master or climb one hurdle, here comes something else that shakes your routine.

Have you ever just been moving along and minding your own business and then out of the blue something happens that in unexplainable? You may ask yourself, why is this happening to me? What did I do that caused me to end up here in this place? What do you do when your trial seems to overtake you, and you feel like there is no resolution to the situation? As a Christian, you are not exempt from having trials. You must learn how to endure, how to make it, how to continue to move on in spite of the hardship.

James 1:4 states, Let perseverance finish its work so that you may be mature and complete, not lacking anything. In order for you to become mature and complete, you must go through the complete cycle of a trial. At the end of the trial, the goal is to be successful in fulfilling the process that God has designed, not lacking anything, and to become whole. In your life as a Christian, you should strive to fulfill the destiny designated for you. When you strive to fulfill your destiny, it gives you the opportunity to seize all that God has planned for your life.

Jeremiah 1: 5 (KJV) reads: Before I formed thee in the belly I knew thee; and before thou camest forth out of the womb I sanctified thee, and I ordained thee a prophet unto the nations.

God was there in the beginning, he will be there through the process and will be there till the end, as you complete your earthly assignments. What has he designed or ordained you to do? Are you doing it? Are you walking in your destiny? Your Purpose, your destiny, your ministry, your assignments will look different from other people's assignments, but they are YOUR assignments that should be embraced and done to the best of your ability.

Let's take a moment to look at a biblical character that experienced various trials that tested his faith, patience and endurance. He also endured tremendous suffering and experienced temptation. I am speaking about Joseph of the Old Testament. He did not experience one trial but had multiple ones. ***Genesis Chapter 37,*** begins to tell the story of Joseph's life. Joseph was seventeen years old and was number eleven out of twelve sons. He also tended flocks of animals with his other brothers. His father, Israel, loved

Joseph more than the other sons and gave him a coat of many colors. This gift was a token of love from his father.

I can imagine that Joseph cherished this coat and was really appreciative of the fact his Father had given it to him. He was very proud of this gift. Now as you may know sometimes when God blesses you, others around you can't handle it. Others may look at what you have and say "Who do they think they are?" From a spiritual stand point, there may be some of you that have haters. That's right haters; they hate to see that God is working it out for you, they hate to see you continue to move through life and surviving. His brothers were very jealous and hated him.

Joseph had a dream, and when he told it to his brothers, they hated him all the more. He said to them, "Listen to this dream I had: We were binding sheaves of grain out in the field when suddenly my sheaf rose and stood upright, while your sheaves gathered around mine and bowed down to it." His brothers said to him, "Do you intend to reign over us? Will you actually rule us?" And they hated him all the more because of his dream and what he had said. Then he had another dream, and he told it to his brothers. "Listen," he said, "I had another dream, and this time the sun and moon and eleven stars were bowing down to me." When he told his father as well as his brothers, his father rebuked him and said, "What is this dream you had? Will your mother and I and your brothers actually come and bow down to the ground before you?" His brothers were jealous of him, but his father kept the matter in mind." Genesis 37: 5-11

God began to deal with Joseph through dreams. Joseph in his immaturity discussed everything in detail from those dreams, and then his brothers began to hate him more. The dream was his parents and brothers would someday come and bow down to him. Lesson learned: Sometimes when God shows you something for the future, you can't share it with everyone. You must operate in discernment in sharing the things of God. As you begin to move through the various stages of life towards wholeness, it involves a process.

The process of moving toward wholeness can be compared to a mathematical term of numerators and denominators. In elementary school, you were exposed to fractions. Within a fraction, the top number is the numerator and the bottom number is the denominator. Similarly, your life represents fractions (episodes or pieces) that move you towards wholeness. Fraction examples of the number four would be: **1/4, 2/4, 3/4,** and **4/4**. The numerator, or top number of these fractions represents (troubles or trials) in life that are constantly changing. The bottom number, or denominator represents the standard or that which is constant, **God**. I will use Joseph's life as an example of how his different life experiences helped him reach his ultimate destiny. Joseph had four specific experiences (that I will discuss as **1/4, 2/4, 3/4**, and **4/4** fractions), which helped him to arrive at God's plan for his life.

"Now his brothers had gone to graze their father's flocks near Shechem, and Israel said to Joseph, "As you know, your brothers are grazing the flocks near Shechem. Come, I am going to send you to them." "Very well," he replied." Genesis 37: 12-13

Joseph was given the destination, Shechem, by his Father. He was going along, minding his own business and obeying his Father's instruction. How many of you have a destination in life that you are moving towards? Have you been given instructions by God to do a particular assignment? Have you ever found yourself in a place that you had not intended to be? If so, where?

And a certain man found him, and, behold, he was wandering in the field: and the man asked him, saying, What seekest thou? And he said, I seek my brethren: tell me, I pray thee, where they feed their flocks. And the man said, They are departed hence; for I heard them say, Let us go to Dothan. And Joseph went after his brethren, and found them in Dothan. And when they saw him afar off, even before he came near unto them, they conspired against him to slay him. And they said one to another, Behold, this dreamer cometh. Come now therefore, and let us slay him, and cast him into some pit, and we will say, Some evil beast hath devoured him: and we shall see what will become of his dreams. And Reuben heard it, and he delivered him out of their hands; and said, Let us not kill him. And Reuben said unto them, Shed no blood, but cast him into this pit that is in the wilderness, and lay no hand upon him; that he might rid him out of their hands, to deliver him to his father again. And it came to pass, when Joseph was come unto his brethren, that they stript Joseph out of his coat, his coat of many colours that was on him; And they took him, and cast him into a pit: and the pit was empty, there was no water in it. Genesis 37: 15-24 (KJV)

His brothers were so jealous of him. This jealousy caused them to commit an act in which they stripped Joseph of his coat. How many of you have ever been stripped of something that was rightfully yours? To be stripped of something leaves your emotions and faith vulnerable. Vulnerability means that you are open to attack or damage. Joseph's coat represented a certain level of protection of his father that was stripped away from him by his brothers.

I can recall as a child that our family home was robbed several times. We were stripped of our personal items. Not only was our personal space violated, but I hated that the individuals had eaten our food in the refrigerator and had literally touched every item in our home. We discovered our dresser drawers overturned, our beds stripped of the linens and trash all over the house. The mental image of seeing our home in this manner was very upsetting. One item that my parents had given me for a gift, a ring made out of a penny was taken in one of the robberies. I loved the ring and remember crying that it was actually gone.

For many years after the robberies, I did not feel safe in our family home. Even though we had gotten a security system installed, I always felt that we would get robbed again. Once I moved from home to attend college, it gave me an opportunity to move beyond the fear of being robbed again, and I was able to eventually move into my own apartment. I can imagine that Joseph was extremely upset that his brothers had stripped him of what was rightfully his. So what do you do when something that is rightfully yours is taken away from you?

Joseph's brothers not only stripped him of his coat, but they contributed to his first fraction, **1/4.** Joseph's **1/4** trial was his **PIT EXPERIENCE.** A pit is a hole in the ground, often sunken or depressed. It is often dark, cold, and empty. Your pit experiences in life sometimes have you feeling alone, with no one being able to quite understand what you are experiencing. Your pit experiences and your times alone may cause you to cry out, maybe as Joseph might have done. First, he was possibly saying, "Hello anyone there, hello help me please, hello get me out of here, hello this ain't funny, hello, hello, hello, does anyone hear me, does anyone care, is anyone concerned?" Imagine him trying to climb out of that cold, dark and lonely place. Your pit experiences are a test of your endurance. Are you able to survive the present conditions that you are in? Are you able to endure the pain of being underneath while others are on top? You can hear what they are saying about you, but they can't begin to understand the pain that you are feeling.

The one thing I love about God is he will sometimes send someone to help you get out of your pit. It could be a family member, a friend or even a stranger. These individuals will pull you out, even when you feel like no one could possibly care. God used my husband to help pull me out of a stage in my life that I was depressed. He did not give up on me but extended a life line when I needed it. God will also use the most unlikely person to pull you out of the mess that you may experience. The story states that Joseph is pulled out of the pit, but he is not totally 100% free. He was sold into slavery. As you begin to reflect, what is your **PIT** experience? How were you able to overcome your **1/4** trial?

_____

_____

_____

Let's move towards Joseph's **2/4** experience. Joseph was given over to the Midianite merchants who, according to **Genesis 37:36,** sold him unto Potiphar. Potiphar was the captain of the guard and one of Pharaoh's officials. **Genesis 39:2,** shows the denominator, God, in action. In Joseph's **2/4** experience, God is present. *It states, The Lord was with Joseph so that he prospered,* *and he lived in the house of his Egyptian master.* Not only was God with him, but Joseph became a successful man, who became Potiphar's personal assistant. Joseph obtained FAVOR! He was put in charge of everything that Potiphar owned. So here the denominator, God, is there with him!! So in spite of any trial that he may face, God is always there!!

So Potiphar left everything he had in Joseph's care; with Joseph in charge, he did not concern himself with anything except the food he ate. Now Joseph was well-built and handsome, and after a while his master's wife took notice of Joseph and said, "Come and sleep with me!" But he refused. "With me in charge," he told her, "my master does not concern himself with anything in the house; everything he owns he has entrusted to my care. No one is greater in this house than I am. My master has withheld nothing from me except you, because you are his wife. How then could I do such a wicked thing and sin against God?" And though she spoke to Joseph day after day, he refused to go to bed with her or even be with her. Genesis 39:6-10

Joseph being a young man with all the power in the land caught the attention of Potiphar's wife. People are attracted to status and position. Some people may associate themselves with you because of the position or role that you may be involved in. Joseph is now experiencing his 2/4 fraction – a trial that will help push him towards his destiny, which is a **TEMPTATION.**

As you may recall, a trial is a test of faith, patience or endurance through suffering or temptation. Temptation is when someone is encouraged to do wrong for pleasure or gain. Some things that tempt one person has no effect on another person. If you struggle with something, the temptation to engage in it becomes escalated at different points in time. For me, my temptation is certain foods.

As I shared with you in an earlier chapter, a temptation for me would be at around 3:00 pm, going into the break room at work, walking by that vending machine and seeing that Snickers candy bar just sitting there waiting to be purchased. It was like it was calling me, Felicia, come buy and eat me now! Knowing that if I chose to give in to that temptation, there would be a temporary pleasure, but the consequence is that it could ruin my healthy progress of that day. Yes, temporarily, I would be satisfied, but there would be a price to pay later. When you give in to your temptations, it can set you back from reaching your potential.

Genesis 39: 7-19 tells the story of Potiphar's wife and how she was very attracted to Joseph. She wanted to seduce him and boldly asked him to engage in sexual activities with her. Joseph was an unmarried young man who was presented with a distraction. This temptation involved a woman who was already married to another man. For him to be with her sexually would have been another level of problems. Don't allow distractions to get you off your life plan. When presented with temptations, respond to them with God's help by saying "NO" to the distraction and fleeing quickly from the situation. One moment of temporary pleasure can lead to a lifetime of pain. Joseph did not accept her sexual advances, and, as a result, she lied on him to her husband about what had happened between them. Potiphar was very furious with Joseph and had him thrown into prison. Have you ever experienced any **TEMPTATIONS**? If so, did you give in or did you flee? What strategies are needed to be implemented to help you flee from future temptations? What are your **2/4** life experiences (your **TEMPTATIONS**)?

_____

_____

_____

Joseph was now experiencing his **3/4** fraction in his **PRISON EXPERIENCE.** So where is, God, the denominator in this season of his life? *In Genesis 39:21, the Bible tells states: the Lord was with him; he showed him kindness and granted him favor in the eyes of the prison warden.* Has anyone ever helped you when you were in a mess? Even in prison, Joseph was still successful. Similarly, you, too, can be imprisoned or locked up mentally, spiritually, physically, or emotionally. What an awesome feeling to be in captivity and still make progress towards an ultimate goal. Is it possible to be successful and confined at the same time? The lesson to learn is to make the most of where you are in spite of the situations that you sometimes face. You can be in physical confinement but still able to do the work of the Lord. God wants you to make the most out of your unpleasant experiences. How will you use those experiences to give Him glory? One way is by sharing your *TESTimony* with others. Remember there is no *TESTimony* without a test. There is no *TESTimony* without the experience of some type of trial!

Genesis Chapter 40 introduces us to Pharaoh's cupbearer and baker that were sent into prison because they had offended Pharaoh. As a result, they were sent to the same prison that Joseph was in. While they were there, they had dreams and did not know how to interpret them. Joseph had an opportunity to hear the details of the dreams, and he used his gift of dream interpretation to explain to them what the dreams meant.

God will sometimes use you, even as you are going through your trials, to help someone else. Don't be so consumed with your own confinement that you miss an opportunity to minister or be used by God to help others. Joseph could have concentrated on his own plight, being consumed with his own pity party and would have missed out in helping them. Do things to help others even when your situation seems bleak. In *Genesis 40:15*, Joseph acknowledges he was imprisoned falsely, but it did not stop him in helping two other prisoners with their situation. In **Genesis 40:21**, the cupbearer was restored back to his original position in society and in **Genesis 40:23**, *after helping him the word states: The chief cupbearer, however, did not remember Joseph; he forgot him.*

Don't depend on others to deliver you out of your trials. You must have faith in God. He is the only one certified and qualified to deliver you! God will deliver in his own timing. For some, the time is short, and, for others, it is longer. For Joseph, two years passed and he found himself still in prison. Have you ever been confined to something and you look around and everyone else around you is free? It seems as though they are enjoying life and have no cares in the world, and you are **STUCK**! It is safe to assume that others came into prison before, at the same time, or even after Joseph arrived there and were possibly released before him. God sometimes chooses to take you through a process in which you are not instantly delivered from a thing. You may go through it for an extended period of time.

The Bible does not say what happened between **Genesis Chapters 40 and 41.** Joseph may have questioned God and might have doubted his abilities. He possibly may have helped other prisoners during this time. We don't know, but what you can learn is that while you are in your prison, others may forget about you, but God remembers you and will deliver you in his own timing.

In **Genesis Chapter 41**, just when you can think the story may end, God intervenes on behalf of Joseph. Two years later, Pharaoh had a dream in which he did not know what it meant. The same cupbearer, whom Joseph had assisted, remembered the situation of his dreams being interpreted by Joseph and told Pharaoh about him. He remembered how accurate Joseph was in helping him during his time of need. ***Genesis 41: 12-14 states, "Now, a young Hebrew was there with us, a servant of the captain of the guard. We told him our dreams, and he interpreted them for us, giving each man the interpretation of his dream. And things turned out exactly as he interpreted them to us: I was restored to my position, and the other man was impaled." So Pharaoh sent for Joseph, and he was quickly brought from the dungeon."***

Your works should speak on your behalf way after you have left the scene. Make an impact wherever you go. You never know how others will remember and interpret your actions in the future. Make positive deposits into the lives of others, so they may withdraw them when needed. When you deposit negative things such as gossip, back-biting, or lies, there are no positive results. When you plant positive seeds such as encouraging words or affirmative statements, others can review those words when they need it the most. Have you ever had a **PRISON EXPERIENCE?** Have you ever been bound up physically, mentally, emotionally or professionally? If so, list your **3/4** experience below:

_____

_____

_____

_____

_____

Joseph interprets the dream of Pharaoh, and, as a result, he was freed and then reaches his **4/4** fraction, **THE PALACE EXPERIENCE.** Joseph was chosen to rule over all of Pharaoh's house and kingdom. Joseph went from his pit experience all the way to the Palace. Each fraction was a part of his life story. He is a great example of when you go through trials and temptations, that if you hold on, keep the faith, the trouble only lasts for a specified time, and there will be victory on the other side. If you just keep moving through life, you will go from being stripped of some things to owning some greater things. So don't worry about it if things have been taken from you wrongly.

"Then Pharaoh took his signet ring from his finger and put it on Joseph's finger. He dressed him in robes of fine linen and put a gold chain around his neck. He had him ride in a chariot as his second-in-command, and people shouted before him, "Make way!" Thus he put him in charge of the whole land of Egypt." **Genesis 41:42:**

What Joseph had lost as a child was given back to him doubled as an adult. The Bible states in **Joel 2:25 (KJV)**, *"And I will restore to you the years that the locust hath eaten, the cankerworm, and the caterpillar, and the palmerworm."* This scripture means that God is capable of giving back to you all that you have lost. Not only did God bless Joseph, while he was in the palace, but God changed the course of living and functioning for his biological family as well. God used Joseph and the power of reconciliation to bring his family back together again when the region was about to experience a famine. God will use your trials to mature you as you become complete and whole. This is obtained as you cultivate your relationship with him. God was with Joseph through every step of his life. Even though his faith was tested, he persevered and was able to overcome his trials. In the end, he lacked nothing, and he received all he needed to be successful for the rest of his life.

The lessons from Joseph's story conclude in spite of the fact that you will have different trials in your life; all of the fraction experiences (**pit, temptations and prisons**) are a part of your journey towards wholeness, your **4/4** experiences. Through your different types of tests and temptations, the constant denominator, which is God, is always there. Through his son Jesus, God tells us in **Matthew 28: 20b (KJV)**, *"I am with you always, even unto the end of the world."* God being the constant in every part of your life will help you in having the patience and perseverance to make it through to the next fraction. Being whole is not just about one aspect of your life, but it is about every part of your life. I finally was able to look in the mirror and say "I am fearfully and wonderfully made!" I took comfort in knowing I was God's child! I was His in spite of what others thought or said about what I should or should not be doing in my life. Once I confronted my own life truths and identified generational patterns that have been passed down through my family tree, my life took a whole new direction, and I have been moving towards wholeness ever since! I decided the outcome or my end result would be different than others before me. I want my life and that of my children to be different! As a result, I was able to move forth with God's ultimate plan for my life. Your journey towards wholeness is not about being perfect, it's about being the best you possible. Your biggest competition should be yourself. You must be better today than you were yesterday! That is the secret in Moving Towards Your Best U!

Step 9: Make It Happen: Moving Towards Your Best U!

Be who you were created to be!

Have you reached your **4/4 PALACE EXPERIENCE** *in life? If so, what have you experienced in that fraction of your life? If not, are you moving towards wholeness?*

Felicia Lucas

REAL DEAL TALK

My journey towards wholeness has not been an easy process. There have been plenty of times in which I had no clue as to what I should have been focusing on or what I needed to do next. I would start a project, would never finish it and would find myself frustrated. I have been with my current employer for over eight years. That is truly a record for me because I would only stay two or so years on my other jobs. I had no idea that I was suffering from a Cycle of Discontentment! I appeared to be happy in life, but I was never satisfied. I would do the job for a little while, started to lose interest and would seek out something else to do. It wasn't the job that was the problem; it was me. I had to reach a place in life just as the scripture says in **Philippians 4:11 (KJV): "For I have learned, in whatsoever state I am, therewith to be content."** *This has been a process to truly embrace the test, trials and temptations as part of my story. I had to do some deep soul searching and make some tough life decisions. When I finally reached that stage in my life within the last five years, I shifted my thinking about what was important in regards to my life, health, marriage, family and my career. I have been able to accomplish so much more in reference to living my life purpose! I can truly say that I am finally content, and I am excited about passionately pursuing God's plan for my life!*

AFTERWORD

"My philosophy is that not only are you responsible for your life, but doing the best at this moment puts you in the best place for the next moment."
-Oprah Winfrey

This book is about my personal journey towards Wholeness. All the good, bad, ups and downs have made me into the woman I have become today. After working through this book, it is critical for you to begin implementing the tips and strategies as soon as possible. Which area(s) of your life needs immediate attention?

- Spiritual
- Emotional
- Physical
- Professional

Being whole in all areas of your life is essential to living out your divine purpose. If any areas are out of balance, it will affect other areas of your life. It is not a good idea to just focus on one area in life and neglect the other areas of your being. Your intimacy relationship with God will bring you closer to obtaining victory in each area of your life. God will help you to keep things in balance as you draw closer to him. The area that needs immediate attention then becomes your urgent priority.

It is important in your planning process to prioritize which area to focus on next. As you have learned, the **K.I.S.S.** plan

(Keep It So Simple) is needed to avoid becoming overwhelmed. Prioritizing requires you to determine what is urgent, important or what you should not give any attention to. It also aids in spending your time doing the right things that are right for you. Once you address your immediate needs, you can begin to look at each of the other three areas in your life and **Make It Happen!**

Let's recap some of key points from each chapter that will aid you in determining your own process of **Moving Towards Your Best U!**

Chapter 1: *Just like when a man proposes to a woman, God proposes to mankind. Have you accepted God's intimacy invitation?*

Chapter 2: *A relationship with God is the most important relationship you can have. Have you begun to cultivate this relationship?*

Chapter 3: *Plans that are simple and easy to follow will increase your probability of success. Your plan is your guide to success.*

Chapter 4: *The sooner one taps into their BTDT (Born To Do This), the easier one's life will begin to move towards operating in Godly purpose. You are an original masterpiece. No one can do what you do, like you do it! Many can try to copy but their extreme effectiveness and relatability is wrapped up into completing their designed purpose.*

Chapter 5: *Choosing to be happy and living to please God will allow you to Move Towards your Best U! Pruning away from unproductive and unfruitful relationships will be a hurtful process. The ultimate result of walking in God's purpose will bring life fulfillment.*

Chapter 6:	Staying in a fixed mindset, not growing or maturing, can stunt one's growth. Don't short change yourself and those around you, for not being willing to change. Movement is necessary. Until you change your mind and move, you will remain where you are.
Chapter 7:	God is the Ultimate CEO (Chief Executive Officer) in your workplace. It is very important to be successful in your career and to operate in the spirit of excellence. God is always watching what you do, so make sure you have his "thumbs up"!
Chapter 8:	The process of waiting can make a person stronger and more valuable. Being delayed in achieving workplace goals, can also provide additional opportunities for you to tap into undiscovered job skills.
Chapter 9:	Your journey towards wholeness includes all areas of your life. Don't just focus on one aspect of life and neglect all the other parts of who you are.

Accepting God's intimacy invitation many years ago is the foundation in which I used to help me to complete this book. I am thankful he placed the dream within me, and I was able to do it. All glory belongs to God for helping me to accomplish this part of my life story. I encourage you to take a personal life assessment and determine your next course of action. Will you implement the tips and strategies shared or will this book end up on the bookshelf in your home or office? Movement is necessary for you to obtain your goals. Your results are only as powerful as your decision to move towards becoming whole. ***1 Corinthians 2:9 (KJV) reads, "Eye hath not seen, nor ear heard, neither have entered into the***

heart of man, the things which God hath prepared for them that love him." Feel free to utilize my contact information in the About the Author Section of the book and share with me your movement progress. I would love to hear about your wholeness journey! ***Get ready to Move Towards your Best U!*** I'm rooting for you!!

ABOUT THE AUTHOR

Minister Felicia Lucas, Inspirational Speaker, Author and Empowerment Coach, is also known as the *Polishing Enthusiast* who passionately and enthusiastically helps individuals who have lost their life luster to become vibrantly new again. From dull and off track, Minister Lucas empowers them to be brilliantly whole by teaching individuals how to grow spiritually and professionally, enhance their relationships and become wonderfully well from the inside out.

Moving Towards Your Best U! – That's her mission, to teach others how to think, do, become and live the BEST life possible. With her **Make It Happen** message, Minister Felicia knows how to motivate people with transformational tools to unleash their BEST lives so they can be happy, healthy and holistically well. She provides empowerment sessions, personal coaching, and motivational talks that inspire others to become their best self.

Minister Lucas, a woman with a heart after God, is the co-founder of **Take It By Force Ministries, Inc.** a 501©3 non-profit community based organization, which empowers individuals to become responsible model citizens within their communities, with her husband, Pastor Kelvin Lucas. Together they are powerfully impacting generations to live out their greatness.

She's a devoted wife of 19 ½ years, mother of three children and committed community activist. Minister Felicia is also the co-founder of **Dominion Tabernacle Church** in Rocky Mount, NC where she happily serves as the Administrative Pastor. Felicia and her husband, faithfully provide practical teachings of the Word of God to individuals from all walks of life.

Minister Felicia loves to give back to her community through speaking to residents at the retirement center, providing job readiness skills in underprivileged neighborhoods and volunteering for the Making Strides against Cancer Walk. Her accomplishments and accolades include, PTA President, Community Mentor at Zebulon Boys and Girls Club & East Wake High School's Ladies of Tomorrow Program. She serves as Vice President of the Rocky Mount Federation of Business and Professional Women's Club Inc., and a member of the Board of Directors for the NC Federation of Business and Professional Women's Club Inc., and she is also the recipient of the 2014 Wake County School's PTA Council Star Award and the 2016 NC Business and Professional Women's Club Career Woman of the Year.

As an accomplished **Business Woman on the Move**, Felicia is the Founder and CEO of **His Glory Creations**, a Christian Publishing Company and **A Moment in Time**, a Wedding Consulting and Special Events Planning Company.

Felicia graduated from the University of North Carolina at Chapel Hill with a B.A. Degree in Speech Communication, and, for over 20 years, she has worked in the Human Resources Field and currently works as a Regional Human Resources Facilitator and Store Manager for a national retailer.

CONTACT INFORMATION:

Website: www.felicialucas.com

Facebook: Author Felicia Lucas

Twitter: @MoveToYourBestU